FEILDEN CLEGG BRADLEY STUDIOS
LEARNING FROM SCHOOLS

Artifice
books on architecture

CONTENTS

FEILDEN CLEGG
BRADLEY STUDIOS
LEARNING FROM
SCHOOLS

PETER CLEGG

INTRODUCTION

A hundred years ago my grandfather, Sam Clegg, helped design a new secondary school in Long Eaton, Derbyshire (Fig 1). It was one of the new generation of secondary schools which was borne out of the 1902 education act which introduced education for all up to the age of 14, an act which sparked the first major school building programme of the twentieth century. He wasn't an architect by training (though he claimed to be one when he signed the plans of his new house) but he worked closely with the County Architect George Widdows to design what was then the most substantial building in the centre of the town. It was inspired, as he was, by the Arts and Crafts Movement, as evidenced by the mural paintings in the Chaucer room and the Milton Room (Fig 2). There are also overtones of Macintosh in the top floor art studio with its northlight glazing. But it is the scale of the building that is most impressive, signifying a new urban architectural typology, with solid and decorated architecture and ecclesiastical overtones. It placed secondary education on the high street at the heart of the community.

from left Fig 1/ Long Eaton County Secondary School, 1909, Architect: George Widdows, © Peter Clegg; Fig 2/ Sam Clegg, teaching in the Chaucer room at the Long Eaton School where he was headmaster, © Peter Clegg; Fig 3/ Tadcaster Grammar School, 1959, West Riding County Architects Department, © Peter Clegg.

Exactly fifty years later my father, then Chief Education Officer for the West Riding of Yorkshire, opened the secondary school that I was to attend. Although it was still called a grammar school it did in fact have a comprehensive intake. It was built on the outskirts of Tadcaster (Figs 3 and 4), a town similar in size to Long Eaton, because there wasn't enough room on the site of the old grammar school. And, like hundreds of other schools built during the second great school building programme of the last century, it was built using a standardised construction system (CLASP) that speeded up both design and construction and just about managed to keep up with the extra provision needed for the baby boomer generation. The structure, cladding and insulation were all minimal, designed to produce low-cost buildings very speedily, but the rate they were produced across the country was formidable. During the mid-1960s the West Riding alone was opening one school a week. They were minimal and barely functional, a series of classrooms and laboratories served by double-loaded corridors and staircases that produced traffic jams at breaktimes. Overglazed rooms overheated in summer and were too cold in winter. The architectural language, though it was undeniably new and different, was hardly inspiring and, though my own school has survived and may well deserve listing as a good period-piece, most of its contemporaries haven't survived because they were so poorly constructed.

Fifty years further on and we come to the third great secondary school building boom. It would be great to think we could learn from past mistakes and produce buildings that not only reflect current attitudes to education, but will prove to have more than a 50 year life by ensuring that they will be flexible to future change in pedagogy and technology. But this time the political situation is very different. It was easy for local authorities to churn out schools when they had relatively substantial budgets and unchallenged executive power. There was also a more desperate need. In the last ten years the provision of schools has been devolved to all kinds of new providers and developers, each of which has been learning from scratch how to programme, construct and commission a new school. This has led to painfully long delivery programmes, exacerbated by lengthy consultative processes and a huge variety of design approaches. But the positive side of this process has been that the nature of school design has been debated from first principles and many of the assumptions about the brief for the buildings have been tested and re-evaluated.

This book is a record of our re-thinking of the idea of a school over the last ten years. From the identity and iconography of a school through to the details of acoustic and energy performance, we have tried to record what has changed, what we have explored and what we have learned. We have also analysed the performance of many of our buildings, sometimes in simple out-turn figures of attainment and attendance, sometimes in more detailed analysis of the way the school has been received by both staff and students. And in some instances we have analysed the energy performance and related that to the database that has emerged over the last decade of new schools buildings.

Fig 4/ Tadcaster Grammar School, 1909, West Riding County Architects Department, © Peter Clegg.

The book is divided into four sections. The first consists of a series of essays, beginning with a discussion of the historical context and looking at a typological approach to school design. We also examine the key issues that all designs need to address: the architectural identity of each new school and the degree of flexibility for future change, and explore various approaches that have been made to introduce a more human scale to what have now become very substantial institutions. We look at breaking down the organisation into what amounts to a series of 'schools within a school', trying to avoid the idea that the school is simply a series of 55 square metre classroom boxes, and thinking more about creating a variety of formal and informal learning spaces.

The second section of the book looks at the comfort conditions in a school through an understanding of environmental technologies: heat, light, air and sound. We examine the approach we have taken to the design of daylighting and ventilation and the acoustical environment of schools, and look at heating systems and renewable energy installations.

The third section also contains a photographic record of eight of our most significant schools, together with a short summary of each one and associated plans and sections. It is intended as a reference base and an appendix to the essays in the first three sections, but also to give a sense of the spaces in use. We feel privileged to have been part of a very creative period of school design.

In the final section we have tried to draw some conclusions from what we have learned by working with teachers and educationalists, from a series of post-occupancy evaluations of our schools and from the experience of ten years and more in the secondary school sector. As we take stock of an extraordinarily creative period in the rethinking of the secondary school environment and we return to a more conventional period of more gradual evolutionary change we have tried to establish some key principles to give direction to future projects. There are always lessons to learn.

HISTORICAL CONTEXT

DEAN HAWKES

THE HISTORICAL CONTEXT

INTRODUCTION

> "Look at these big isolated clumps of buildings rising up above the slates, like brick islands in a lead coloured sea.
> The Board Schools.
> Lighthouses my boy! Beacons of the future! Capsules with hundreds of bright little seeds in each, out of which will spring the wiser better England of the future."

This is Sherlock Holmes, speaking to Dr Watson, as they looked out of the window of a train near Clapham Junction at the end of the nineteenth century. The skyline of the city had been transformed by the programme of school building that followed the passing of the 1870 Elementary Education Act. These tall, handsome, brick and glass buildings laid the foundations and were symbols of a new age, from which we may trace the development of school architecture to the present day.

Schools have been built in England since the Middle Ages. In the standard history of the subject, Seaborne cites the foundation of Winchester College in 1382 as the starting point and describes a rich history of schools, large and small, from then up to the latter years of the nineteenth century.[1] But it was the growth of large urban populations in the nineteenth century that led to the 1870 Act. This obliged all local authorities in England and Wales to investigate educational provision in their area and, if there was a shortfall, to undertake the construction of new schools financed by a charge on the local rates. As a result there was a new wave of school building across the country in which key principles and practices were established.

This essay begins with the 1870 Act and outlines the principal events and movements that have informed school design in Britain up to the recent past. The narrative focuses on the design of larger buildings, what became secondary schools, and is structured around three specific themes: Typology, Architectural language and Environmental principles.

THE 1870 ACT AND THE BOARD SCHOOLS

In 1871 The London School Board appointed ER Robson as its Chief Architect and within three years Robson published his book *School Architecture*[2]. This quickly

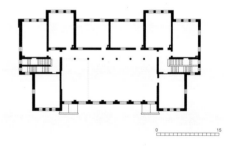

0   15

p 6 St George's, Classroom, © The Environmental Tradition, Dean Hawkes, copyright (© 1996) and Taylor & Francis, reproduced by permission of Taylor & Francis Books UK.

above Fig 1/ ER Robson, Jonson Street School, Hacknet, Plan, © Feilden Clegg Bradley Studios.

from left Fig 2/ ER Robson, Bellenden Road School, Southwark, © Elain Harwood; Fig 3/ Lockwood and Mawson, Feversham School, Bradford, © Historic England; Fig 4/ Woodhouse and Willoughby, Moss Side Board School, Manchester, © Elain Harwood.

became a *de facto* design manual. The dominant plan type that Robson illustrated was the 'Hall Plan', with classrooms arranged around a central hall, or in the taller buildings, two halls one above the other (Fig 1). There was much debate on the question of appropriate architectural style for non-sectarian education. London, under the influence of the School Board architect, ER Robson, opted for the 'Queen Anne' style (Fig 2) in which surfaces of London brick were punctured by large, white-framed windows. At this period Robson was in partnership with JJ Stevenson, who was a leading member of the Queen Anne movement.[3] In other cities, other styles were adopted. For example Birmingham and Bradford clothed their schools in the Victorian Gothic revival (Fig 3) and in Manchester, where Gothic has been the dominant style for the city's new civic and institutional buildings[4], paradoxically chose a pragmatic, undecorated style (Fig 4)[5].

Whatever the stylistic preferences, the buildings' questions of environment, of health and hygiene, were fundamental to these buildings. In those days before efficient electric lighting, emphasis was placed on the provision of good daylighting. Chapter IX in Robson's book contains a detailed discussion of "School Seats and their Lighting", in which suitable window dimensions are calculated in relation to the rooms they serve. His recommendation was that the ratio of window to floor area of a classroom was 1:5. In Chapter XV, similar precision is given to the provision of 'Warming and Ventilation'. Here the recommended solution for larger buildings was a 'Plenum' system. In this, warmed air from a basement plant room circulated through a system of supply and extract ducts incorporated into the fabric of the building to be finally evacuated

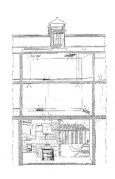  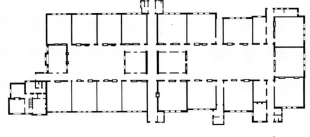

from left Fig 5/ Plenum Heating Diagram, ER Robson, © Feilden Clegg Bradley Studios; Fig 6/ Martin and Chamberlin, Somerville Street School, Birmingham, © Oosoom at Wikimedia Commons; Fig 7/ Martin and Chamberlin, Conway Road School, Birmingham, Plan, © Feilden Clegg Bradley Studios.

through a rooftop vent (Fig 5). These were usually clothed in Queen Anne cupolas or gothic finials, as the different styles required. In Birmingham, the firm of Martin and Chamberlain who were architects for all the Board Schools, constructed tall and often strikingly unadorned ventilation towers (Fig 6). At Conway Road School, built in 1900 to accommodate 1,050 pupils, the organisation of the whole plan is strikingly modern, based on two parallel spine walls that accommodate all the air ducts (Fig 7).

THE 1902 EDUCATION ACT

In 1902 a new Education Act transferred responsibility for schools from the school boards to local authorities and introduced a distinction between elementary and secondary education. In the latter, provision was made for teaching in science and practical subjects that required specialised laboratory sand workshops, in addition to conventional classrooms. As the cities and towns extended into new suburbs, school sites became larger and this released school design from the constraints of earlier densely urban locations. Many schools continued to be based on the 'Hall Plan' typology, but the more generous sites in the suburbs allowed the development of new types that allowed better natural ventilation. The principal of these were the 'pavilion' plan (Fig 8) and the courtyard plan (Fig 9).

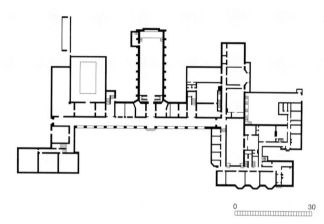

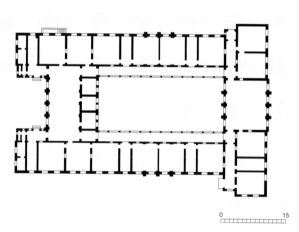

from left Fig 8/ Leonard Stokes, Lincoln Grammar School, Plan, © Feilden Clegg Bradley Studios; Fig 9/ Urban Smith, Letchworth Elementary School, Plan, © Feilden Clegg Bradley Studios.

To coincide with the passing of the new Education Act, Felix Clay who was appointed chief architect to the newly established Board of Education, published *Modern School Buildings, Elementary and* Secondary.[6] This was modelled on ER Robson's 1874 volume, that was in effect the design manual for the new type of schools. As with Robson the need to provide good daylighting is emphasised. In reviewing prescriptions for determining the sizes of windows, Clay confirms the suitability of Robson's recommended ratio of 1:5. He disagrees, however, with Robson's suggestion that cills should be five feet above the floor, arguing that children should be able to enjoy a view out when at their desks. Now, in the twentieth century, artificial lighting is given explicit attention and, although gas and oil lighting is discussed, the advantages of electric lighting are already compelling and the subject is discussed at length. The recommendation is that one 16 candle-power incandescent lamp should be allowed for each 50 square feet of classroom floor area.

Fig 10/ Plenum Ventilation system, Felix Clay, © Feilden Clegg Bradley Studios.

The continuing importance of the environment in schools is stressed by the inclusion of a 30-page chapter on 'Ventilation and Heating'. This includes a detailed discussion of air quality and of the processes of air circulation within classrooms. Central heating was now almost universal and alternative systems are described. The 'Plenum' system continued to be recommended and is illustrated with a new 'system diagram' (Fig 10). Clay describes the installation at Conway Road School in Birmingham, illustrated above, as an example of the latest practice. This had a 7-foot diameter fan, driven by a 4-horsepower gas engine that propelled air through the system in both winter and summer, delivering 6 air changes per hour in the classrooms. Clay describes the success of the system, following a visit on a warm summer day, "... the air was certainly of the pleasantest". The Board of Education required that classrooms should

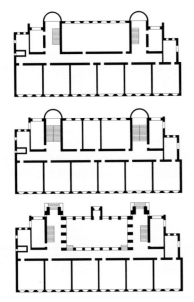

be heated to between 56° and 60° Fahrenheit and Clay observed that, " ... generally speaking a room that is at 59° or 60° at the opening of the school will be found comfortable". As a comparison Clay pointed out that the standard in America was 70° F, which he attributed to the fact that American houses were more generally "mechanically heated" than was common practice in Britain.

Architecturally this was an interesting period in Britain. Alastair Service identified two predominant and contrasted stylistic ideas, Edwardian Classicism and Edwardian Free Design.[7] Many, perhaps the majority, of schools were built in a conventional 'neo-Georgian' style. Cassland Road School in Hackney (Fig 11) is typical of these, but this was also the time when the Arts and Crafts Movement, or the 'English Free School', was at its height. George Widdows, County Architect of Derbyshire, built a number of Arts and Crafts inspired schools in the county (Fig 12) and, in Lancashire, Edgar Wood and JH Sellars, major figures of the Arts and Crafts in the region, built the impressive, almost proto-modern, Durnford Street School at Middleton in Lancashire, completed in 1909 (Fig 13). Pevsner recognised the originality of the building when he wrote, "Here, by experiment, two Lancashire architects of no great renown got as near as anyone in England to the most progressive American and European work of 1900–1914."[8] The school, whose plan was a variant on the 'Hall' type, combined Infant, Junior and Senior departments with a total of 1,000 pupils. Environmentally the building was as advanced as its architecture with a low-pressure hot water heating system, with electrically powered extract ventilation through the three tall towers. In Glasgow, at exactly the same time, Charles Rennie Mackintosh's Scotland Street School (1903–1906) (Figs 14 and 15) brought his unique sensibility to bear on school design. This was also a 'Hall' plan and was heated and ventilated by Boyle's Air Pump System.[9] As was now common practice, the building had electric lighting.[10] There are striking similarities, both architecturally and environmentally, between Scotland Street and Mackintosh's Glasgow School of Art, which was under construction at the same date, although the Art School had a fan-driven ventilation system.[11]

BETWEEN THE WARS

School building between 1919 and 1939 was constrained by economic difficulties. Elain Harwood describes the period as "a missed opportunity" architecturally.[12] Nonetheless there were some important developments. The Hadow Committee, set up by the Board of Education to consider a wide range of questions on education, published an important series of reports between 1923 and 1933 that set out the latest thinking on matters such as the development of the curriculum and the equipment of schools. The Building Research Station, which was established in 1921, brought scientific approaches to many aspects of building construction and design and these were brought to bear on schools.[13] Members of the Station's staff contributed to the

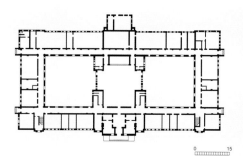

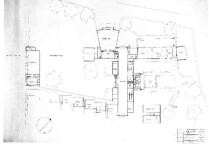

top row from left Fig 16/ Granger and Leathart, King George V School, Southport, Plan, © Feilden Clegg Bradley Studios; Fig 17/ City Architects Department, High Storrs Grammar School, Sheffield, © Historic England; Fig 18/ SE Urwin, Bottisham Village College, Cambridgeshire, © Dean Hawkes.

bottom row from left Fig 19/ Gropius and Fry, Impington Village College, Cambridgeshire, Aerial Perspective, © RIBA Library Drawings Collection; Fig 20/ Gropius and Fry, Impington, ground plan of the school buildings and grounds, © RIBA Library Drawings Collection; Fig 21/ Gropius and Fry, Impington, Classroom Block, © Dell & Wainwright / RIBA Library Photographs Collection.

RIBA report "The Orientation of Buildings" (1933) that included a discussion of the orientation of school. This was a theme that was to become an important influence on the planning of schools. Typologically and stylistically the approach to design in this period was predominantly conservative, with quite formal pavilion or courtyard planning, traditional construction and architectural language (Figs 16 and 17). Younger British architects, however, became interested in European and American developments, where the ideas of architectural Modernism were beginning to influence school design. SE Urwin, County Architect of Cambridgeshire, adopted a Dutch-influenced brick language, in the manner of Dudok's work in Hilversum, for the first village colleges commissioned by Henry Morris the influential Director of Education for the county (Fig 18). The high point of Morris', work occurred in 1939 with the collaboration between Walter Gropius and Maxwell Fry at Impington Village College, where the language of the Bauhaus was given an English accent (Fig 19). The informal plan (Fig 20) was a striking departure from the formality and symmetries of earlier designs, creating sheltered open spaces between the wings and allowing a southerly orientation for the main classroom block (Fig 21). This had extensive glazing with sliding doors that opened onto outdoor teaching areas. All this was prophetic of what was to come in the decades following the Second World War.

THE POST-WAR YEARS

The 1944 Education Act was one of the most significant events of its time. It promised "secondary education for all" and introduced a three-tier system of secondary education: grammar schools, secondary technical schools and secondary modern schools. In architecture, school building quickly became the focus of a fundamentally new approach. Andrew Saint has argued that school building in the post-war years combined,

> "... many things... the Modern Movement, a puritan strain in British philosophy and design, the needs, constraints opportunities and organisation of post-war reconstruction and the triumph of fresh thought about childhood, teaching and learning."[14]

The building programme was promoted by the establishment of large and ambitious local authority architects' departments, most notably, in the early years, that of Hertfordshire County Council. A further fundamental influence came from the Architects and Building Branch (A&BB), established in 1948 at the Ministry of Education.[15]

The outcome of this was an architecture that was rational and straightforward, that, "… made no great architectural reputations and produced no masterpieces in the conventional sense."[16]

Nonetheless these buildings, with their compositional informality and lightness of construction and environment, were as expressive of the social and political ideals of the time as were Robson's London Board Schools for their generation.

The A&BB published a series of Building Bulletins that covered a wide range of topics related to school design. These defined fundamental principles and provided precedents for practice by undertaking exemplary 'Development Projects' that influenced school design for four decades.[17] Particularly relevant here are Bulletins:
- Building Bulletin 2 New Secondary Schools, 1950.
- Building Bulletin 8 Development Projects: Wokingham School, 1956.
- Building Bulletin 17 Development Projects: Secondary School, Arnold, 1960.

Building Bulletin 2, which was written by Margaret and David Medd, who were leading members of the A&BB team, set out the general principles that were to guide secondary school design.[18] At a time of economic constraint much emphasis was placed on planning to tight space standards, but within these the Medds were able to articulate principles that moved English secondary school design in a new direction. These emphasised the importance of allowing the plan to reflect the educational brief, rather than observe architectural notions of symmetry and form. At the same time they stressed the importance of natural lighting and of good ventilation, the environmental agenda.

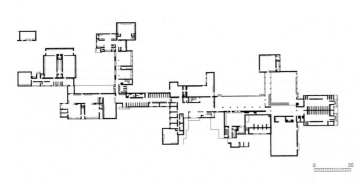

0   20

from left Fig 22/ Architects and Building Branch, Wokingham School, Plan, © Feilden Clegg Bradley Studios; Fig 23/ St Crispins Secondary School, Wokingham, © Architectural Association Photo Library.

The school at Wokingham was designed by the A&BB to demonstrate the translation of principle into practice. Both schools were on suburban sites that were typical at this time. The plan (Fig 22) was dispersed in nature, following the principles of Bulletin 2. It shared the informal typology of Gropius and Fry at Impington Village College, with distinct blocks, or pavilions, accommodating specific functions. From the beginning there was an interest in 'modular' construction and many schools were constructed using 'systems' of repetitive elements, with exposed structural frames, infill panels and flat roofs (Fig 23).

This was a period when quantitative environmental standards had a significant influence on designs. In 1946 the Building Research Station published its Daylight Factor Protractors.[19] These provided a relatively simple means to compute levels of daylight and this enabled specific standards to be set. In 1945 the Ministry of Education ruled that classrooms should have a minimum Daylight Factor of 2%, with a recommendation that 5% should be provided, if possible. The effect of this was that some schools were over glazed, with consequential problems of visual glare and winter heat loss and summer heat gains. In response the level was fixed at 2%.[20] The direct effect of these requirements may be seen in the science laboratory at Wokingham, where the sidelighting from the window is supplemented by a continuous rooflight at the rear of the room in order to maintain a uniform distribution of daylight (Fig 24).

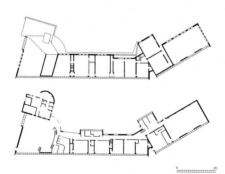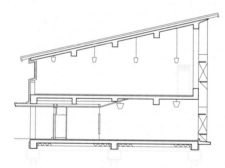

top from left Fig 24/ Elmslie Morgan, St George's School, Wallasey, Solar Wall, © The Environmental Tradition, Dean Hawkes, Copyright © 1996 and Taylor & Francis, reproduced by permission of Taylor & Francis Books UK; Fig 25/ St George's, Classroom, © The Environmental Tradition, Dean Hawkes, Copyright © 1996 and Taylor & Francis, reproduced by permission of Taylor & Francis Books UK.

bottom from left Fig 26/ St George's School Wallasey, Plans, © Feilden Clegg Bradley Studios; Fig 27/ St George's Wallasey, Cross Section of Classroom Block, © Feilden Clegg Bradley Studios.

Late in the 1950s, a seemingly unlikely source made an important contribution to the history of school building in Britain. Elmslie Morgan was the assistant borough architect of Wallasey a town on the Wirral peninsular, just across the river Mersey from Liverpool. St George's School, completed in 1961, was the first school in Britain to make a calculated attempt to capture solar energy as the primary source of heating. This building (Figs 25–27) was one of the first in which the principles of what we now call 'sustainable design', were central to its conception. The entire organisation of the building follows from its environmental objectives. The linear plan allows all rooms to be oriented to the south and the cross-section, high to the south, low to the north, with its striking 'solar wall', expresses the principle of maximising solar gains.

The building achieved 'iconic' status when Reyner Banham discussed it at length in *The Architecture of the Well-tempered Environment*.[21] Although the 'solar' element is the building's most striking feature, its environmental strategy has a number of other, complementary elements. The structure combines a high level of thermal insulation with considerable thermal mass. The solar wall, which is 9 metres high, consists of two glass membranes, 600 millimetres apart, with elements of thermal mass in the void at the locations of storage rooms and staircases. Tilting opening lights allow controlled ventilation in the classrooms. Morgan assumed that artificial lighting would be in use during the winter months and included the heat gain from tungsten lamps in his calculation of heat balance. To ensure this, the daylight level is below the 2% standard of the day. In addition the heat gains from the occupants, the pupils, are included in the calculation of thermal balance.

The building's performance was comprehensively monitored by researchers at Liverpool University.[22] This work shows that the building operated effectively without recourse to the auxiliary heating system that had been installed as a precaution. Winter temperatures were generally within normal comfort standards and there were no recorded instances of overheating in summer. The principal problem that was identified with the building was that the low ventilation rate failed to remove odours from the dining hall and gymnasium. Despite its relative success, the building failed to influence wider practice. This may have been partly due to the reports of ventilation problems, but it may equally be due to the rigidity of the linear form, determined primarily by the needs of solar access, in contradiction of the educational and social preoccupations of the A&BB.

LOW-ENERGY DESIGN

By the end of the 1970s low-energy design was receiving a great deal of attention in Britain, not least in relation to school design, and its importance was given official approval with the publication in 1981 by the Department for Education and Employment of Design Note 17, *Guidelines for Environmental Design*, which formally linked environmental performance and energy use.[23] An important contribution at this period came from academic research in environmental design being carried out in schools of architecture. Some schools, such as Cambridge, collaborated directly with local authority architects' departments in studying the performance of existing schools, in Essex, and in the development of design principles for new school buildings, with Hampshire. Others, including the Welsh School at Cardiff and the Bartlett at University College London, contributed to official publications and Design Bulletins.

In 1994 the Department for Education published Building Bulletin 79, *Passive Solar Schools: A Design Guide*.[24] The department's earlier disapproval of St George's, Wallasey was finally overcome by its inclusion in the Bulletin's brief chapter on 'Historical Background', although even now it was noted that, "some occupants of the school complained of stuffiness".

The Guide summarises the principles of passive solar design and presents an economic and cost analysis of no less than 35 completed passive solar designs and detailed Case Studies of 17 of these. 13 of the 17 Case Study buildings, and all seven of the non-primary schools, featured an atrium. At the time atria had become a familiar part of many building types.[25] The Bulletin presented a simple typology of atria (Fig 29) that defined alternative relationships with adjacent spaces. A properly designed atrium is itself a useful and comfortable space. It can also work as an environmental buffer to adjoining spaces and can help to promote effective natural ventilation in a building. All of these qualities are valuable in a school building.

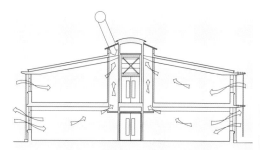

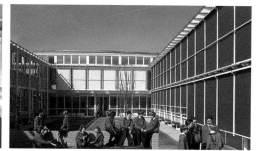

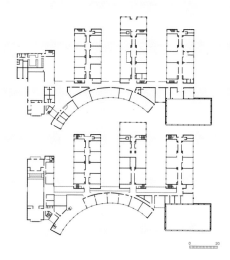

top from left Fig 29/ Cabot City Technology College, Section, © Feilden Clegg Bradley Studios; Fig 30/ Cabot City Technology College, Facade, © Feilden Clegg Bradley Studios; Fig 31/ Cabot City Technology College, Laboratory Interior, © Feilden Clegg Bradley Studios.

bottom Fig 28/ FCBS, Cabot City Technology College, Bristol, Plans, © Feilden Clegg Bradley Studios.

These virtues are shown in FCBS's Cabot City Technology College in Bristol that was selected as a Case Study in the Bulletin, which also incorporates the other passive elements of conservatory, direct gain and solar shading. On a south-facing slope, the plan (Fig 28) focuses on a north-south facing linear atrium. The two-storey teaching blocks open from this with east-west-facing facades. The cross-section of the teaching blocks permits stack ventilation at both levels (Fig 29). The section also shows the different design of the elevations in response to orientation. The north west elevations are unadorned, but those that face south west have external fixed and moveable shading to protect against the afternoon sun. These began to influence the language of the building in which environmental devices were given clear expression (Fig 30). There is an interesting link back to the Medd's work at Wokingham in the first floor science laboratories, where, in each building, sidelight is supplemented by top lighting at the rear of the space (Fig 31).

THE NEW CENTURY

When the Labour government came to power in 1997 education was at the top of its political agenda. Too many schools were failing their children; too many buildings were in a dilapidated condition. It took several years to formulate an ambitious strategy embodied in the City Academies Framework in 2002 to look radically at the vision for new schools to replace those in the worst condition. Exemplar designs were commissioned by the then Department for Education from FCBS and eight other renowned practices and many of these were translated into designs which broke the mould of conventional secondary schools.

Two years later an even more ambitious scheme was launched. Building Schools for the Future (BSF) was set up to rebuild or renovate all of the secondary schools in England over a 15 year period. This in turn led to a re-evaluation of space standards, the use of information technology, and the active encouragement of designers to transform the whole process of education. There was a renewed excitement in more open-plan teaching that became a byword for a while in the 1970s and a determination to break out of the straightjacket of teaching classes of 30 children in a 55 square metre room. At the same time there was a recognition that the last major phase of buildings from the 1960s often failed in terms of their environmental criteria, too much solar gain and heat loss, and not enough acoustical isolation and absorbtion, so these issues were addressed in new Building Bulletins issued by the renamed Department for Education and Skills, and a Government Taskforce on Zero Carbon Schools looked at ways in which the carbon emissions for new school buildings could be rapidly reduced. This is the point at which the project work of this book begins and investigates a range of new buildings which were a response to these architectural and environmental challenges.

After just over a century in the modern history of school buildings in Britain a vital perspective is becoming clear. From the beginnings, with the 1870 Education Act, the architecture of schools has been explicitly concerned with the physical environment in which children are to be educated, and with the technological means by which this may be achieved. In pursuit of this aim, and in response to prevailing educational theories, specific building typologies quickly evolved that reconciled all the elements of programme and technology. Then, the question of architectural language has been addressed in seeking to give expression to the ideals that informed the project.

The last ten years of new buildings have enabled us to look again at the architectural theory and environmental science that have always underpinned the design of our secondary schools. The last century of secondary school building has seen an increase in comfort standards and demands for lower energy consumption. Educational pedagogies have come and gone, open-plan has ebbed and flowed, progressive teaching has cycled with a 'back to basics' approach but at the heart of our schools is a need to provide buildings that provide for the physical, emotional, spiritual and intellectual education of our children. The best of those buildings have endured the test of time and are still with us. There is always more to learn from them.

1. Seaborne, Malcolm, *The English School: Its Architecture and Organization*, Vol I, n 1370–1870, London: Routledge & Keegan Paul, 1971. The history of schools in the following hundred years is covered in a companion volume, Seaborne, Malcolm and Roy Lowe, *The English School: Its Architecture and Organization*, Vol II, 1870–1970, London: Routledge & Keegan Paul, 1977.

2. Robson, ER, *School Architecture*, London: John Murray, 1874. Facsimilie edition, Leicester: Leicester University Press, 1972.

3. See Girouard, Mark, *Sweetness and Light: the Queen Anne Movement*, 1860–1900, Oxford: Clarendon Press, Oxford, 1977.

4. See Stewart, Cecil, *The Stones of Manchester*, London: Edward Arnold, 1956.

5. These stylistic variations are discussed and illustrated in Harwood, Elane, *England's Schools: History, architecture and adaptation*, Swindon: English Heritage, 2010.

6. Clay, Felix, *Modern School Buildings, Elementary and Secondary,* London: ET Batsford, 1902.

7. Service, Alastair, *Edwardian Architecture: A Handbook to Building Design in Britain 1890–1914*, London: Thames and Hudson, 1977.

8. Pevsner, Nikolaus, *The Buildings of England, South Lancashire*, Harmondsworth: Penguin Books, 1969.

9. Robert Boyle & Son began supplying ventilation systems for buildings and ships in Glasgow in the 1880s. By 1899 they also had offices in London, Paris, Berlin and New York. Their 'Air Pump' system used the natural buoyancy of air rather than mechanical propulsion. The firm published a manual, *Natural and Artificial Methods of Ventilation*, 1899.

10. University of Glasgow, "Mackintosh Architecture: Context, Making and Meaning", www.mackintosh-architecture.gla.ac.uk, accessed 29 September 2015.

11. See Cairns, George, "Glasgow School of Art", Charles Rennie Mackintosh Society, Newsletter No 66, Winter/Spring, 1995, Glasgow.

12. Harwood, *England's Schools*, 2010.

13. Lea, FM, *Science and Building: a history of the Building Research Station*, London: HMSO, 1972.

14. Saint, Andrew, *Towards a Social Architecture: The Role of School Building in Post-War England*, New Haven and London: Yale University Press, 1977.

15. Saint, *Towards a Social Architecture*, 1977.

16. Saint, *Towards a Social Architecture*, 1977.

17. A complete list of Building Bulletins published between 1945 and 1974 is given in Seaborne, Malcolm and Roy Lowe, *The English School: Its Architecture and Organization*, Volume II, 1870–1970, London: Routledge & Keegan Paul, 1977.

18. See Saint, *Towards a Social Architecture*, 1977.

19. Dufton, AF, "Protractors for the Computation of Daylight Factors", DSIR Building Research Technical Paper No 28, London: HMSO, 1946.

20. See Hopkinson, RG, P Petherbridge and J Longmore, *Daylighting*, London: Heinemann, 1966.

21. Banham, Reyner, *The Architecture of the Well-tempered Environment*, London: The Architectural Press, 1969.

22. The monitoring is summarised in Hawkes, Dean, *The Environmental Tradition: Studies in the Architecture of Environment*, London: E & FN Spon, 1996.

23. Department for Education and Employment, "Guidelines for Environmental Design", Design Note 17, The Stationary Office, London, 1981.

24. Department for Education, "Passive Solar Schools: A Design Guide", Building Bulletin 79, London: HMSO, 1994.

25. See Saxon, Richard, *Atrium Buildings: Development and Design*, London: The Architectural Press, 1983.

FEILDEN CLEGG
BRADLEY STUDIOS
LEARNING FROM
SCHOOLS

THE
ARCHITECTURE
OF SCHOOLS

THE ARCHITECTURE
OF SCHOOLS
TYPOLOGY

Graham McPherson, better known as Suggs from the 80s band Madness, was speaking about his education in a tough post-war North London Comprehensive school. He recalled corridors "so long it took ten minutes to walk between classes: In that ten minutes you were either made or broken". The experience of schools for children is often defined by what happens between lessons and outside the classroom and it is the nature and organisation of the 'in-between' spaces that creates or destroys a healthy social environment in a school. Many schools built during the second expansion of secondary education in the 1960s were conceived of as campus environments, a series of self contained buildings often based around subject areas linked by corridors or covered walkways. These schools contained an extraordinary amount of wasteful circulation, and necessitated long periods of wasted time moving between lessons: armies of children on the move.

The only advantage of campus style schools was that they created spaces between buildings that could provide a variety of usable and separated outdoor spaces for play or for learning. The possibilities of attractively landscaped courtyards however often became neglected areas of tarmac.

The campus typology has been replaced by a variety of more condensed organisational layouts. We can see the school as a city in miniature. Streets and squares, cafes and market halls, become the corridors and gathering spaces, the dining halls, libraries and communal spaces of a vital community. One mark of a successful school is that it should maximise the usefulness of its 'streets and squares', making social spaces that work rather than circulation spaces that alienate.

In analysing our work over the last ten years we have distinguished a series of organisational patterns. These emerge from site constraints, our reactions to the brief and the pedagogical aims of the school. They can be categorised into four major typologies which we have labelled courtyard, street, atrium, and "superblock". They all have their particular characteristics and advantages, and over the last ten years we have explored all four approaches. Every school is unique and no single typology presents clear advantages that enables it to emerge as a distinct preference. Clarity of organisation however is the key to creating a coherent and legible school environment and is often the starting point of a complex design journey.

p 18 St Mary Magdalene Academy, © Hufton+Crow.

COURTYARD

above The central cloistered courtyard at Northampton academy, © Amos Goldreich.

opposite Typology diagrams, © Feilden Clegg Bradley Studios.

Courtyard schools derive from many historical precedents. The cloister of a medieval abbey and the 'quad' of an ancient university are both spaces we associate with learning and contemplation. Courtyards make outdoor space the heart of the school, and can create a sense of security and community around the occupation of that captured space. The surrounding buildings can look in and look out, as the school engages with itself or the outside world. The circulation route can be inside or out, connected to the central space or running behind a series of classroom spaces that surround it, but there is always the opportunity of fair—weather short—cuts. Many pupils and teachers value the fresh air break between classrooms, and escaping from the constraints of corridors can avoid the problems of overcrowding and pupil traffic jams. It is always useful having a variety of routes in order to enable—or indeed avoid—chance encounters. As a combination of indoor and outdoor routes the courtyard plan can therefore be very efficient.

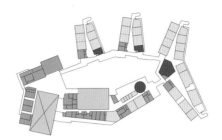

AT NORTHAMPTON ACADEMY, the courtyard takes its inspiration from the expressionist architecture of the german architect Hans Scharoun, whose work included many educational institutions. Here we broke down the mass of the school into a series of clustered classroom buildings around an organically shaped courtyard. This space becomes the heart of the school, analogous to the city square, formed by colonnaded edge of buildings. A generous first floor circulation route—wide enough to encourage social learning and small group work—links all the school and provides views out into the central courtyard or into the double-height teaching hallways that provide a focus for small groups and creates departments of related subject disciplines. At ground floor level the circulation around the outside of the space is sheltered by the upper floor corridor saving building costs and sheltering the entrances to each cluster building. The change in level of half a storey across the canal courtyard adds to the dynamics of the open space that is bounded by the pavilion buildings and first floor links. One of the benefits of the breaks between the pavilion is that there are open views between the courtyard and the landscape beyond, maintaining the sense of enclosure but with glimpses of the world outside.

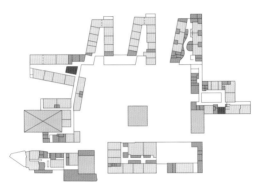

AT TOR BRIDGE HIGH SCHOOL in Plymouth the courtyard idea suggested itself partly from the necessity of phasing of the school building and partly because of the need to link a series of different schools onto one campus. Tor Bridge is an 'all-through' school—a campus that contains primary and secondary schools and a school providing for 72 children with special educational needs. Also linked into the courtyard circulation are a range of community facilities, including a public library, out-of-hours sporting facilities, a museum exhibition area, youth centre, nursery and theatre. The new buildings were built in a series of five phases around the existing buildings which were then demolished to make way for the central courtyard space. A central shared communal facility offers flexible space for all and subdivides what would otherwise be too large a space at the centre of the school. Like Drapers', the changes in level in the courtyard add interest and provide ways of defining the separation between the surrounding buildings.

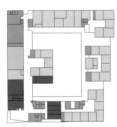

DRAPERS' ACADEMY follows a conventional cloistered courtyard pattern with generous covered circulation along a brickwork colonnade that wraps around three sides of the courtyard space and provides access to ground floor teaching clusters and staircases to upper floors. On the fourth side are the main communal spaces where the circulation runs inside and the centrally placed science department (one of the schools' specialities) protrudes out into the courtyard. The land slopes away to the east leading down to the playing fields and the building massing responds accordingly starting from three stories on the west and stepping down to one-storey at the east to let light into the courtyard and afford views out and over the lower buildings.

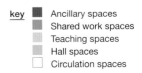

key — Ancillary spaces
Shared work spaces
Teaching spaces
Hall spaces
Circulation spaces

STREET

above A two-storey street at the Samworth
Enterprise Academy, Leicester, © Peter Cook.

opposite Typology diagrams, © Feilden Clegg
Bradley Studios.

FW Sanderson, the pioneering science teacher and founder of Oundle school referred
to school buildings that "should be built more in the manner of museums, with long
commodious galleries and well lit side chapels as workrooms". The commodious
galleries all too often have become reduced to meagre corridors. Redefining the
principal circulation route as a gallery or a street elevates the means of circulation
to a defining idea that gives the school its character. The conceptual idea can vary
from an open space along which functions are arranged in a linear fashion, to a fully
enclosed grand circulation route forming the spine to a single building.

A single street would be uncomfortably long to provide access to all the rooms
needed in a large secondary school and it is logical therefore, following on from
the analogy of the street, to develop side streets and squares and plan an 'urban
strategy' for the whole school. This can work well as a means of linking clusters
of classrooms organised on a departmental or pastoral basis. Linear strategies
can work well when the site suggests the form of layout and when a virtue can be
made of the 'ends' of the street: ie in terms of providing entrances and principle
community spaces.

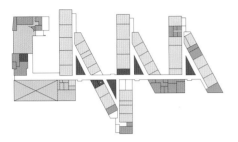

BRISTOL CITY ACADEMY was a challenge in terms of phasing the new school around the existing buildings whilst keeping everything operational. In all there were seven phases of development which in the end resulted in a simple linear format — a main street linking the main entrance and all the communal facilities through to a series of triangular shaped clusters of classrooms each located off the main street. The principle street is occasionally double-height, with bridges sailing overhead, and alternates between looking into open courtyard space between the clusters and atria at the centre of each cluster. As with the Northampton diagram no part of the circulation feels like a conventional double-loaded corridor, the circulation spaces are either designed to provide the commodious circulation that Sanderson sought, or they are top-lit open spaces, acting as social learning areas surrounded by classrooms.

AT THE SAMWORTH ENTERPRISE ACADEMY in Leicester we returned to a more conventional corridor format but enhanced the functionality of the spaces by dropping light into them and furnishing them to series of breakout spaces which could extend the classroom teaching into the corridor. We have discovered that the functionality of these open spaces very much depends on the skills of the teacher and the age of the children. Younger children can be reasonably well supervised but there have been problems with older children not able to be adequately supervised in the open spaces at the upper end of the school. Leicester has an unusual intake with a 2 form-entry primary and 4 form-entry secondary up to key stage nine. We were inspired by the simple idea of the child's journey along the linear path of the school, flowing back and forth to and from the central axial route which contains the principle spaces of the school — the library, assembly hall, the splendid kitchen facilities which are the speciality of the academy, and a Church of England church, which is embedded in the heart of the school near the main entrance.

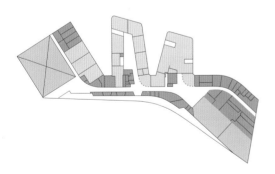

AT THE BRIGHTON ALDRIDGE ACADEMY the curved linear plan came from the shape of the site that could be built upon without demolishing the existing buildings until the new ones were complete. But the site also enjoyed the most extraordinary south-facing views which we were determined to take full advantage of. Here the linear plan takes on its own subtle curvature, modelled on the topography and geology of the ridge of the North Downs as it runs from the hall and dining facilities at the west end near the main entrance to the sports facilities at the east end. Both end sections have community uses beyond school hours: the central section is a more private series of classrooms arranged in teaching clusters around shared spaces.

key   ■ Ancillary spaces
       ■ Shared work spaces
       ▨ Teaching spaces
       ▨ Hall spaces
       □ Circulation spaces

ATRIUM

above Part of the ETFE covered atrium at Highfields Humanities College, Blackpool, © Will Pryce.

opposite Typology diagrams, © Feilden Clegg Bradley Studios.

Atria grew up out of nineteenth century museums and railway stations before becoming part of the language of commercial offices and shopping malls and then being assimilated into schools. Even within a school setting, they retain a grandeur, a sense of commercialism and an architectural significance which some teachers feel is at odds with the human scale nature of education. They can be very useful in terms of enhancing daylight and ventilation and provide a luxurious sense of space but they have also been criticised for poorly designed acoustics and exaggerating the institutionalisation of schools.

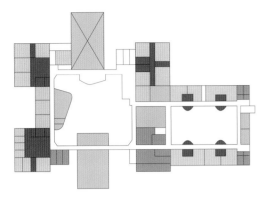

THE EXEMPLAR SCHOOL we designed for the Department for Education was focused around a central Atrium uniting all the secondary school spaces, with a junior school courtyard to one side. We were intrigued by the idea of creating a visible identity of the whole school and clusters of classrooms around it. The concept of enclosing a very large space gave us the opportunity that we found a lot of headteachers were asking for but the standard schedule of spaces could not deliver—namely the creation of a space large enough for the whole school to gather. We were intrigued by the drama of a large central space and its potential as an exhibition or performance venue surrounded by the three storeys of theatrical gallery spaces all round, and we were excited by the potential for activities beyond the curriculum—clubs and societies, cafes and dining spaces— and the creation of an enclosed space that was representative of the wider community that the school served.

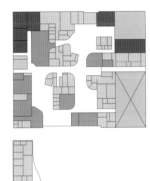

AT HIGHFIELD HUMANITIES COLLEGE in Blackpool we did manage to stretch the width of the circulation spaces to form two spaces that read much more as communal atria rather than merely circulation. Highfield is a school that specialises in the humanities, so the design of the communal spaces and the inclusion of passively supervised social learning areas which would help develop interpersonal relationships between children were a key driver behind the organisational design, and the choice of an atrium led solution. We were also concerned however about creating a totally introverted sense of space within the atria so at each level each space has two social areas known as 'inspiration hubs' which overlook the atrium but also provide visual and physical links to the outside emerging as balconies breaking through the outside walls. Capturing this extra space within a finite budget meant making a few sacrifices. There is a row of spaces through the centre of the plan that do not have outside walls—but these are primarily spaces such as music practice rooms on the ground floor, some practical science spaces on the intermediate floor which are mechanically ventilated and can cope without natural light. And the atria spaces themselves have relatively low-cost finishes internally and an economical covering of inflated transparent plastic (ETFE) cushions.

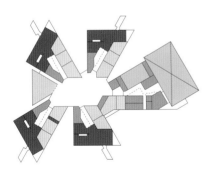

AT THAMESVIEW SCHOOL the concept of classroom clusters around an atrium was pulled apart so that each cluster has its own identity and the communal atrium is the space they all intersect. It becomes a 'great hall' leading out into a series of more independent year based smaller schools each with their own degree of independence and identity—a home base for around 200 pupils of the full age range of the school. This experimental approach to the organisation of the school also extends to the pedagogy. Much of the space is open-plan with each school having its own 'kinaesthetic lab' providing practical facilities for a wide range of subjects, and access direct to landscaped spaces between the separate schools.

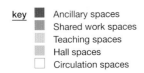

key ■ Ancillary spaces
     ■ Shared work spaces
     Teaching spaces
     Hall spaces
     □ Circulation spaces

SUPERBLOCKS

above Aston University Engineering Academy: A new type of University Technical College occupying a tight urban site in Birmingham, © Steve Mayes.

opposite Typology diagrams, © Feilden Clegg Bradley Studios.

Over the last decade of school building, there has been an ever decreasing budget cost per square metre for state funded schools which has led to a rationalisation of plans and a simplification of the organisational design. One of the simplest ways to reduce cost is to reduce the external envelope area of the building which leads to more condensed plan forms and has created a new typology—one we have christened the 'superblock'. Our atria schemes were moving in this direction anyway, particularly on tight urban sites such as Paddington, and in more recent schemes reducing the ratio of wall to floor area has become a principle driver of design solutions. The advantages, besides cost efficiency, are that a reduced envelope reduces heat loss, and the building footprint is reduced on already constrained sites. The disadvantages can result in poorer quality natural lighting and greater need for mechanical ventilation as plans get deeper. In terms of organisational planning the challenge is to create a sense of clear organisation within a box of a building, and introduce natural light from above and key views out of circulation spaces that otherwise could become mean and introverted. Externally the challenge is one of defining the nature of the box, and creating external playground spaces without the benefit of enclosing walls that emerge from more disaggregated design solutions.

ASTON ENGINEERING ACADEMY occupies a relatively small site fronting onto a busy 4 lane highway in the centre of Birmingham, surrounded by industrial sheds and a post-industrial canal. The building rises to 4 storeys high giving it significant presence, and an urban 'shop window' for engineering education along the edge of the dual carriageway. A narrow central atrium provides a daylit canyon like space through the centre of the building, with a suspended central stair linking the dining space, hall, library and study spaces on the ground floor with the teaching spaces and engineering laboratories on each side. The atrium also provides access to 'homebases' on each floor rising up through the building.

THE PLYMOUTH SCHOOL OF CREATIVE ARTS is another institution that breaks the mould of standard secondary schools, both in age range and curriculum. It accepts children from age 4 to 16 and delivers education solidly based in art, craft, design and media, and is sponsored by Plymouth college of Art. It occupies a triangular shaped space, surrounded by roads and inhospitable buildings in a largely post-industrial landscape. Our response was to create a superblock which was bold and colourful; it rises from two to four storeys and announces itself to the street through a fully glazed entrance leading straight into the cafe style dining area and the main hall. A street carves its way through the block from south to north illuminated by lightwells and large expanses of glazing each end. Much of the teaching space is open plan, and enclosed spaces have glazed walls breaking down the conventional solid barriers between classroom spaces.

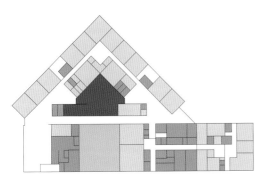

AT WILLIAM PERKIN SCHOOL in Greenford, West London, the superblock becomes triangular in plan and Like Redbridge—four storeys high. Also like Redbridge, the Sports Hall becomes a separate extension to the east. The main block is penetrated by a series of interlinked triangular light shafts, letting light all the way down though the building and containing a series of running staircases. Despite being a four-storey deep plan building, the sense of daylight, dappled and reflected as it cascades down through the building, gives a strong sense of daylight in the building despite the fact that there are a number of classrooms which do not have windows direct to the outside. The internal rooms tend to be those which require mechanical ventilation and acoustic separation (eg music and seminar spaces) or require low levels of light or task lighting (IT and laboratory spaces). The entire school is made of cross laminated timber, which adds warmth to the reflected light where it is exposed within the light shafts.

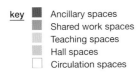

key
■ Ancillary spaces
■ Shared work spaces
Teaching spaces
Hall spaces
□ Circulation spaces

HYBRID SCHOOLS

Of course many schools are based around hybrid typologies—superblocks with atria, linear schemes which bend around and almost become courtyards, making them difficult to categorise. Here are a few that benefit from a combination of ideas but still retain the clarity of a planning diagram that helps with the clarity of the organisation, grouping spaces by subject areas, or daily patterns of use, providing a sense of the identity of the school and organising the efficiency of the circulation. The decision on the overall strategy of these hybrid solutions generally comes from the shape of the available site.

AT ST MARY MAGDALENE ACADEMY, Islington the brief was for an 'all-through' school, ie one which would cater for pre-school children (3–5 year olds) through to sixth form (16–18 year olds) all on one site. The school's sponsor talked about the metaphor of a river in the planning and organisation of the school, and this linear theme is picked up in the circulation from the main Liverpool road entrance along an east west axis to the primary school entrance one-storey higher at the western end of the site. The Primary school has its own western entrance and its own identity whilst benefitting from the common architectural culture of the whole site. It has a more intimate scale and its own playground, with external teaching spaces next to every classroom. The secondary school is based around a four-storey atrium block with circulation all round the central space and the library and faith room forming part of a captures volume in its centre. The school halls form a separate block at the front of the site where they offer sports facilities (including a dramatic rooftop sports pitch) and gathering spaces to the local community.

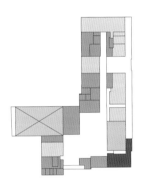

CHELSEA ACADEMY in London occupies the tightest school site we have ever been asked to build with its site being dominated by the Lots road power station to the south and a series of terraced houses to the north and east. The building form respects the height constraints of neighbouring properties so it rises from two storeys at the north to five storeys at the south, even including a basement level in the centre. Every part of the site is built upon, so play areas are all located on the rooftops. At Chelsea we were asked to develop an organisational strategy that was demarcated into three key curriculum areas—science and maths, arts and performance, and humanities. This led to the concept of the building being organised around three lightwells—mini atria, each with their own internal stair and all three linked to an internal street at ground floor level running from the front to the back of the site. The clarity of the plan, with a single major circulation route and ground floor level and two alternative routes at first and second floors enables this very densely packed site able to accommodate the demands of a 1,300 pupil school.

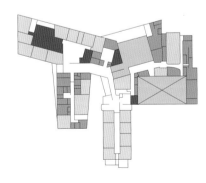

AT TUDOR GRANGE ACADEMY in Worcester the organisational strategy was determined by the site constraints which included the retention and refurbishment, of approximately 30% of the buildings of a former school on the site. New buildings were constructed immediately adjacent to the old to maintain as much open space as possible and provide a new frontage and identity for the school. Typologically the layout consists of a series of classrooms clustered around what became known as 'lead lesson' spaces where several teachers could team—teach up to 90 pupils at once—the open plan approach encouraging a multitude of pedagogical approaches. The clusters all plug into a central rooflit 'heartspace' which in turn links to the retained classrooms and sports hall. Typologically therefore Tudor grange has the compact advantages of a superblock, but with a series of wings that ensure that all classrooms have views to the outside world.

key   ■ Ancillary spaces
     ■ Shared work spaces
     ▨ Teaching spaces
     ▨ Hall spaces
     □ Circulation spaces

THE ARCHITECTURE OF SCHOOLS
IDENTITY

Fig 1/ The timber cladding of the sports hall, with a subtle symbol of the fish, cut into the timber boarding, creates a dynamic elevation onto Liverpool Road, Islington, © Hufton+Crow.

The first generation of secondary schools that grew out of the 1902 Act were tall and significant, their gothic verticality rising above their surroundings and proclaiming them as pillars within their communities. When the post-war population retreated to the suburbs the schools followed them and became rambling horizontal campus buildings in playground and parkland settings. The most recent generation of school buildings have struggled to find appropriate identities but there is a desire from most schools to re-emerge form a more suburban landscape and be seen once again as a centre for the community they serve.

The possibilities offered by the school sites are many and varied. Quite often however when building new buildings to replace an existing school the siting is confined to areas which are second best, with the existing buildings occupying the best part of the site and remaining until the new buildings are finished. Sometimes it is a question of creating a new frontage or making the best possible connection to buildings that are retained and refurbished.

Often the larger scale communal facilities, sports and assembly halls, are those spaces which, because of out of hours use, are located close to the front of the site, and therefore give the school its identity. This means creating a front facade out of what is often a series of windowless spaces. At St Mary Magdalene the logical site organisation suggested that the sports hall should form the main facade of the building on Liverpool Road. We had lengthy discussions with our sponsor clients who were a Church of England organisation and wanted some kind of subtle symbolism built into the main facade of the building. We created a timber clad box where the projection on the timber fins subtly reads in the shape of a 'vesica' or can be as a fish (Fig 1), both having Christian symbolism. Our clients commented that they thought it was very appropriate that you would have to look carefully in order to see the image—it is only with a sense of enquiry that one finds religious fulfilment!

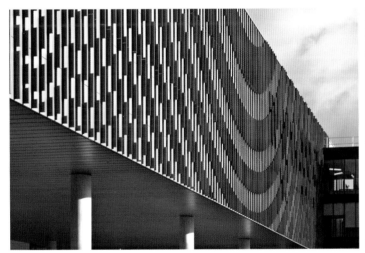 

We used a similar technique at the Isaac Newton academy at Redbridge, West London. Here the school site is tucked away down a side street and the buildings are almost invisible. But the decision to raise the sports hall above ground created an intriguing portico entrance, and the cladding of the blank facade of the hall itself was modified to reveal a series of Newtonian rings, a physical phenomenon in which an interference pattern is created by the reflection of light between two surfaces. Altering the depth of the vertical seams in the gold coloured metal cladding provided an intriguing patterned surface that could be read from the entrance to the side street and in effect provided a street presence for the school (Fig 2).

Sometimes combining schools with other public facilities can enhance the street presence. At Bristol City Academy, a sports science based school, the sports hall is double the normal size and has an immediate street presence that announces the school. In the suburbs of Leicester the unusual integration of a church into the school (the local diocese being one of the sponsors) provides immediate impact at the front entrance (Fig 3).

New schools on very tight urban sites often form part of the urban enclosure of the street. But getting 1,000 or more children through the doors efficiently each morning

from left Fig 2/ Notching the projecting fins that form part of the cladding on the sports hall produces a pattern of 'Newtonian rings' on the elevation at the Isaac Newton Academy in Redbridge, © Timothy Soar; Fig 3/ The circular form of the Church embedded in the Samworth Enterprise Academy in Leicester makes clear the dual identity of the building: a church integrated into a school, © Martine Hamilton Knight.

and afternoon becomes a spatial challenge. Many schools have more than one entrance to help facilitate this. At the new academies at Chelsea (p 93) and at Plymouth, both buildings have a real street presence, both create a slight inflexion behind the pavement line to cope with the rush hour numbers but both also have 'back doors' which in effect mean the school is opened up to become part of the urban streetscape during the times when pupils are arriving and departing. Only security concerns have prevented us from taking one more step that we have done in higher education facilities of seeing the ground floor realm of the school become a part of the public realm of the city.

Of course, sometimes because of site constraints the school is set back from the street frontage and the definition of the entrance becomes a different kind of problem. At Tudor Grange in Worcester we created an entrance plaza embraced by two wings of the building one of which reaches up and out towards the main street entrance. At Brighton it is the curved glass wall that runs the full length of the building's public facade (Fig 4). At Highfields in Blackpool where the school is set back from the entrance, the cladding of the building became the dominant feature of the building.

The elevations here are bold but not alien in its context, using traditional materials while drawing references from both the seaside and domestic architecture of the area. Blue and green glazed tiles are arranged in a series of wave like patterns running all round the four sides of the building, creating a fluid and colourful identity that is restrained and classic in its detail and proportion (p 111).

External identity can define a building in the public perception but the internal identity is more significant for the users. The organisational typologies discussed previously can help define this, but the key spaces are often what remain as memorable about the school. With Northampton it is the central courtyard (p 73) as well as the upper floor corridor around it. At Bristol it is the central street running right through the school (Fig 5); at Paddington the slots of space provide vertical links through the school (Fig 6). Our research on the spaces that children like or dislike has helped us recognise what works and what doesn't, both within rooms and within the public 'internal' spaces that often define the school. This has been limited to only a few schools in detail but it does show that architectural space and aesthetic quality score more highly than we had imagined amongst what children think of their school.

from left Fig 4/ Brighton Aldridge Community Academy where the curved frontage with its inviting collonade provides the entrance to the school and its architectural iconography, © Richard Chivers; Fig 5/ The linear street at Bristol with double-height spaces alternating with bridges, © HBG Construction; Fig 6/ Vertical slices of space at Paddington bring daylight and connectivity to the internal spaces, © Hufton+Crow.

THE ARCHITECTURE
OF SCHOOLS

SCALE

Fig 1/ The grand scale of the central dining hall of the Samworth Enterprise Academy in Leicester is at the centre of a school serving 5 to 16 year old children, © Martine Hamilton Knight.

Why do we have 30 children in a class, or why for that matter are there normally around 1,000 to 1,200 children in a typical secondary school? There are answers to do with management of the education process and efficiency of delivery but we very rarely question the assumptions of a typical brief from the Education Funding Agency. During the first decade of this century the questions were asked and different options emerged.

The group of 30 probably came from the fact that that was the maximum number you could sit at nineteenth century style desks and those at the back could hear the teacher and hopefully see the blackboard during 'chalk and talk' lessons. We found that most teachers would inevitably prefer lower class sizes but only in science subjects did we occasionally find the numbers were reduced to 25. With different teaching methods we found some teachers and educationalists were enthusiastic about spaces which could contain team teaching in groups of 60 or 90, such as the common areas we designed into Tudor Grange or Hastings Academies. Some felt that smaller groups of children could be trusted to work in an adjacent space, part of say a teaching 'corridor' that we developed for Samworth Academy at Leicester (Fig 2). But not all teachers appreciated the flexibility that was provided for them. Thamesview school in Kent for instance was designed to a 'transformational' brief which asked for very large open plan spaces with screens between class areas. Many teachers felt this was imposed upon them and reacted against the design. Interestingly when we talked to the children they seemed to appreciate the school more.

What we remain confident about is that teaching and learning is not confined to the classroom and we have observed that when attractive social learning spaces are provided then they will be creatively used. The era of the double-loaded corridor with no use other than for circulation came to an end when we were given an extra 10% of space to design with. Unfortunately the recent return to pre-2002 standards has meant that our ability to create social spaces that can have a real function is disappearing.

The change in scale from primary to secondary school has always concerned teachers and educationalists. It is responsible for a dip in performance for 11-year-olds at key stage 4, and there are genuine concerns that the social development of children, and their relationship to their school environment is damaged during this transition. This is discussed in more detail in section 3. We have explored various strategies for reducing or eliminating this problem. One strategy is to integrate or at least co-locate primary and secondary schools on one site. We explored this through our study of an Exemplar 'all-through' school for the then Department of Education and Science in 2005, and translated this into a number of real projects. St Mary Magdalene in Islington (p 83) and Tor Bridge High school both take children from 3 through to 18; the Samworth Academy Leicester (Fig 1) and the Plymouth Academy of Arts (p 137) from 4 to 16. All of these have separate zones for younger and older children. These schools don't solve the problem for everyone. Secondary schools tend to have an intake of 4 to 7 classes per year (120 to 210 children) whereas primary schools tend to have a smaller intake of 3 to 5 classes per year (90 to 150 children) to reduce the overall size of the institution, so 'all-through' schools do still tend to have some feeder primary schools to add to their secondary intake. But for those lucky enough to benefit from the smoother transition the evidence is that the shock of the larger school is considerably reduced.

Other benefits also accrue. The sharing of cross-school facilities such as catering and IT can bring economic benefits and the primary school children will have the benefit of sports and assembly halls for older children. But our experience of the 'all-through' schools we have designed is that the teaching remains generally separate, ie the benefits are more in terms of co-location rather than integration.

The overall size of the secondary school is dependent upon the number of classes or forms per year and is generally influenced by the size of the school it may be replacing or predicted demand for places. Most of the 11 to 18 schools we have worked on generally end up accommodating between 1,000 and 1,400 pupils. They are big and often impersonal institutions: most secondary school teachers will teach around 250 different children every week.

Fig 2/ Samworth Enterprise Academy Leicester where the corridors were designed as spill out space for small group meetings, © Peter Cook.

In 2009 we did some work with James Wetz (Figs 3, 4, 5), a former headteacher from a large comprehensive school in Bristol who became very interested in the underperformance of our secondary schools when compared to international standards and why so many children become disengaged from their educational provision at secondary school age. Wetz became concerned by the revelation that 40% of young people leaving school in Bristol in 2004 without any GCSE qualifications had achieved above average results in English, mathematics or science at primary school. These were young people who had to manage complex emotional and social changes in their lives and he concluded that the organisation and design of secondary schools had failed to meet their needs.

He looked at the success of the small school movement in the USA, particularly the Boston Pilot schools where numbers were restricted to less than 400 pupils, and also at Scandinavian precedents such as the Danish Folkeskole, always less than 500. In these schools the teachers only have to form relationships with 75 children: they know them better and can more easily attend to individual needs: education becomes more child focused.

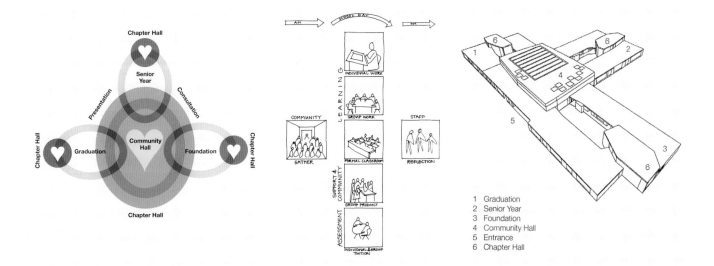

1 Graduation
2 Senior Year
3 Foundation
4 Community Hall
5 Entrance
6 Chapter Hall

So we developed a brief for James and a prototypical concept design that was based on a small school with 375 children with three clusters of classrooms (each for around 25 children) around what was christened a 'chapterhouse', a small assembly hall that would accommodate 150 children in the foundation years (7 and 8) the senior years (9 and 10) and 75 in the graduation year (11). Each school would have some specialist rooms and its own community hall but if one assumed that sports facilities were provided elsewhere then the overall area is only marginally greater than the 8.3 square metres per child set out in current government guidelines. The complete study was published in James' book *Urban Village Schools: Putting relationships at the heart of Secondary School Organisation and Design* published by the Calouste Gulbenkian Foundation in 2009.

Interestingly we found that the Academy provider ARK worked to a similar brief, breaking down the institutionality of a large school of 1,080 children into a series of smaller schools each with its own front door, its own communal space for gathering and eating, and its own external area for relaxation. At Redbridge Academy we worked

from left Fig 3/ Diagrams from the urban village school study. The diagram of a small secondary school with 375 children divided into smaller classroom clusters, © Feilden Clegg Bradley Studios; Fig 4/ Organisational diagram representing three intimate courtyards around a community hall; Fig 5/ Sketch axonometric of small school components.

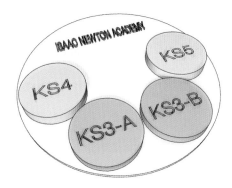

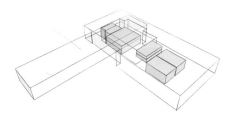

to their brief which required two schools of 360 children and one of 270, plus a sixth form. The relatively small site and the complex interrelationships between the spaces meant that the overall building was like a three dimensional puzzle with different integrated and overlapping volumes for the different schools (Figs 7, 8, 9).

Most large secondary schools have an organisational strategy that manifests itself as a series of smaller volumes of classroom space, organised either by year groups, or by departmental or faculty areas. Traditional organisations can become like the 'silos' of academic departments at universities which leads to greater specialisation and limits the integrated teaching that is regarded as highly successful in primary schools. So most schools tend to group departments into three or four faculties which can fall into obvious categories such as science technology and maths, languages and humanities and visual and performing arts. Clustering different subject areas can shake up the curriculum in an intriguing way but specialist spaces generally need to be clustered by subject area and become fixed curriculum areas with general teaching areas retaining more flexibility. In some schools we have tried to separate and give identity to the clusters. Identity can be provided by opening up the connecting corridor to create a shared space and connecting the floors with a stair and double-height space to unify the classrooms which face onto it. We first used this 'V shaped' spatial arrangement at Bristol where each cluster opens up to provide social learning space, enriched with IT facilities. The clusters connect onto a double-height street. At Northampton the clusters become more like separate buildings with a corridor connection at first floor only sheltering cloistered connections below. At Tudor Grange the corridors widen out to become the shared spaces that give group identity to subject areas.

But it is the social spaces and circulation routes that most easily define our buildings. A classroom is a classroom: it is important that it can function to house 30 children in a variety of activities, but it is limiting architecturally. It is the spaces in-between that give the school its interior identity, that can be adapted for individual study or small group work, that can extend the range of educational experience in both teaching and learning activities. We need to recognise that spaces for dining and social interaction, spaces for play and for contemplative study are all part of the schools' educational experience. And ultimately if teaching and architecture are working together, we ought to be able to provide places where children feel safe, and where anxieties are contained, where bonds of attachment are formed to create a sense of community which works against the alienation that has characterised so much of our schools.

opposite Fig 6/ Isaac Newton Academy at Redbridge, the central courtyard provides access to different 'schools within a school', © Timothy Soar.

from top Fig 7/ Isaac Newton Academy at Redbridge follows the ARK approach to providing four schools within the keystages of a conventional secondary school, © Feilden Clegg Bradley Studios; Fig 8/ The tight site at Redbridge meant we had to produce an interlocking three-dimensional puzzle of the different schools, © Feilden Clegg Bradley Studios; Fig 9/ Communal spaces for each school within the overall volume, © Feilden Clegg Bradley Studios.

THE ARCHITECTURE OF SCHOOLS

SPACES

Fig 1/ The two-storey dining hall provides the ground central entrance space for Tor Bridge High school, © Craig Auckland Fotohaus.

The best schools are buildings which generate a sense of community and are a part of their community. In an ideal situation the majority of children live within walking distance and the schools are buildings which are seen as a focus for the immediate community, and offer much more than education for children during school hours. Their facilities are often open for a 16 hour day: key spaces such as sports and assembly halls are regarded as community facilities, they need to be more outward facing and the school security system needs to allow for different uses for different parts of the building at different hours of the day and week.

The 'big' spaces in schools are those designated in the standard Education Funding Agency brief for assembly, for dance and drama, for sports and for dining (Fig 1). The latter has always caused problems and has never been given the space it deserves as a genuine community space. The interactive design process with many schools involves deciding how to get the best out of these spaces by combining them often with elements of circulation and sometimes with each other. Multifunctionality is essential but often involves compromises.

THEATRES AND AUDITORIUM SPACES

Very few schools now require or can accommodate whole school assemblies. They find the time taken to gather and disperse the children isn't worth the effort. But whole year assemblies are common or assemblies of vertical pastoral care 'houses' of 200 or so children. So for many schools the traditional assembly hall has become more of a theatre and performance space. In most of the exemplar schools illustrated, we have conjoined a 200 square metre flat floor hall with retractable seating, with a 90 square metre drama room with an acoustic sliding folding partition between the two.

This seems to work well and give reasonable flexibility allowing the two spaces together to function as a theatre and each space on its own to be used for smaller drama classes or lectures. We have found that partitioning is difficult to manage and maintain. It has been known to lose its acoustic isolation qualities, but, on balance, the flexibility can be beneficial. Additional capacity and theatricality can be introduced by connecting the retractable seating to a balcony at first floor level as at Chelsea Academy (Fig 2). At William Perkin School (p 127) we pushed the capacity further with two drama spaces and a wider assembly hall providing for a capacity of 700.

DINING SPACES

The educational value of dining is often overlooked. For many children who never sit down to a meal at home, school can add a new social experience, and for children who have no sense of nutritional value the food they are offered at school can fill a gap in their understanding. Some schools take the dining experience very seriously whilst others reduce the seating area to a minimum and go for multiple sittings as short as 15 minutes to churn through the dining process. In the former category the

Fig 2/ The ground floor level circulation space provides additional seating working down into the assembly hall in the basement at Chelsea Academy, © Tim Crocker.

ARK academies often decentralise eating into different schools within a school, which causes logistical problems, though in the Isaac Newton Academy in Redbridge they opted for a more centralised facility which doubles up as a whole school assembly space. The addition of a drama building to one side and balconies on three sides provides a space for 500 children at the heart of the school, but requires a lot of time for furniture management to change from one use to another.

By contrast at Tor Bridge High school, an 'all-through' school with as many as 1,450 children on one site the dining experience is given pride of place in a grand hall that is seldom used for anything else, and sections of it are managed for children of different ages: it is the one place where all children come together, and works as a communal heart to the campus. The same is true of the Samworth Academy at Leicester (Fig 3) where food technology is one of the specialisms and the dining hall was designed to be big enough for all the children to eat together with a very well fitted out kitchen and servery area. Unfortunately the acoustical isolation was omitted as a cost cutting exercise and the space is too noisy and disruptive for the younger children who now eat separately in their own part of the school. Dining areas are inherently noisy: at

another school a glazed partition was retrofitted between the cafe space and the atrium to reduce acoustic disruption.

Dining areas spilling out into atria spaces can work, though it is really important to ensure the necessary mechanical ventilation systems are designed to ensure there is no contamination of food smells that end up permeating throughout the school. Outside spaces can complement internal dining areas and reduce congestion, particularly when covered or sheltered to provide a little more weather protection. At Northampton academy the dining spills out into the sunny side of the central courtyard (p 81), and at Tudor Grange (Figs 4 and 5) the dining area at the end of one wing seems to work very well as a space that removes the associated noise from the centre of the space and allows the dining activity to spill out into the landscape.

SPORTS SPACES

The ubiquitous four court sports hall is generally the largest space in any school. Larger secondary schools also need other facilities such as a gym or fitness suite but the sports hall provides the big box space. It generally doesn't work to use the space for any other activities because of damage to the sprung floor, though some schools do use the space

above from left Fig 3/ The central dining space at Samworth Enterprise Academy, Leicester gives the school a strong identity around its food specialism, © Martine Hamilton Knight; Fig 4/ The dining area at Tudor Grange Academy is located at the end of one of the wings where the seating can spill out into a collonade and terrace, © Craig Auckland Fotohaus.

opposite Fig 5/ The dining area at Tudor Grange Academy is located at the end of one of the wings where the seating can spill out into a collonade and terrace, © Craig Auckland Fotohaus.

for examinations. There is a tendency for sports halls to be very utilitarian spaces and the requirements for completely flush detailing and slightly sprung finishes up to at least 2.4 metres to avoid injuries. Daylighting and views are often sacrificed on cost grounds but introducing either or both humanises the space (Figs 6 and 7).

Acoustical absorption is also important to reduce internal noise levels, and careful isolation to avoid transfer. Both of these can be achieved with perforated timber linings. Sports halls can sometimes be difficult to integrate into a school layout. In tight urban sites we tend to use the roof space to provide a multi-use games area which is the equivalent in size of the four court area below. Although it is costly to create buildings above the wide span of a sports hall we have found it logical to build accommodation such as changing facilities below, and in the case of Redbridge school which was really tight for outside space the raised volume of the sports hall provides carparking underneath and also provides a dramatic new identity for the school.

LIBRARIES AND LEARNING SPACES

Traditionally libraries had symbolic value as the repositories of knowledge, representing the heart or the head of the school. We tend to locate them in significant spaces, in the centre of an atrium space as in Mary Magdalene Academy (Fig 8) or on the street frontage at Chelsea (p 93).

As learning resources become more digitally based, libraries have followed suit, books are tending to disappear, and IT based knowledge can be accessed anywhere. Some schools have decentralised learning resources into departmental 'hubs' but have found it difficult to maintain computer terminals in unsupervised spaces, though in other areas where the terminals are overlooked the distribution of learning terminals seems to work well. It is not difficult to imagine that the proliferation of iPads and mobile devices will eventually mean that in schools, like universities we will see children using digital technology anywhere and everywhere. At Plymouth School of Creative Arts this is already beginning to happen (Fig 9), and when one child complained recently that he would miss one of his favourite classes if he went home as recommended because of an infectious illness, his classmates figured out a way to stream the content of the class direct to his iPad!

opposite Figs 6 and 7/ The importance of daylight and views to humanise sports halls. View from the outside at Chelsea Academy and from the inside at Samworth Enterprise Academy, Leicester, © Tim Crocker (top), © Martine Hamilton Knight (bottom).

from left Fig 8/ The central library within the atrium at St Mary Magdalene, Islington, © Hufton+Crow; Fig 9/ IT terminals line the edges of one of the atria at Plymouth School of Creative Arts, © Hufton+Crow.

Some of the feedback from some children, particularly those in the first year of secondary school however is that they enjoy the traditional quietness of a library as an escape from the hurly-burly of the rest of the school, and there is a strong argument for preserving areas of peace and quiet. We also find that sixth form study areas are both respected and well used both for quiet learning and IT based study. Over the years we have tried a series of experimental computer based learning arrangements of tiered seating but we have generally found that a series of back to back tables works the best with easy circulation all round.

SCIENCE SPACES

Science teaching went through a tactical rethink eight years ago inspired by the government run Project Faraday taskforce. The suggestions that emerged from that looked at reconfiguring laboratory spaces as well as creating demonstration spaces which encouraged the use of informal raked seating areas, lecture and presentation spaces which could take one or two classes at a time. We installed these at a couple of schools and they seem to have had some success in changing the nature of teaching. At Drapers' (Fig 10) which is a science based academy the laboratories are

focused around a space like this which, alongside an adjacent greenhouse space is located off the main circulation route and helps establish a presence for the science specialism of the school.

Within more conventional laboratory spaces the layouts are always a keen subject for debate between science teachers. Some prefer a room with two ends, one for experiments and one for conventional classroom teaching. We have in other areas installed benches around a central space occupied by the teacher (Fig 11). The most flexible and economic solution we have found consists of service pillars around which benches can be arranged in a variety of different ways. Once again flexibility seems to be the key to ensuring the building remains responsive to changes in teaching methodology.

CLASSROOM SPACES

Over the last ten years we have had many debates with educationalists and teachers about creating more flexibility than is normally provided by the standard 55 metre square classroom. Design solutions have ranged from 150 metre square 3-classroom spaces to the provision of greater flexibility through the incorporation of sliding folding

from left Fig 10/ The central open-plan presentation space at Drapers' Academy forms a focal point to the science based curriculum at the school, © Timothy Soar; Fig 11/ Science pillars in laboratories can provide a variety of arrangements like this arena-like layout at Tudor Grange Academy; © Kier Construction.

partitions between classrooms. In other schools we have squeezed classroom sizes down slightly in order to generate more useful shared areas around which classrooms have been clustered, or widened corridors to make 'breakout' spaces. The success of these experiments has been mixed. In one school where the idea of team teaching in a more open plan environment was stipulated by the local authority it did not find favour with staff members who preferred their own classroom spaces. The fact that the sound absorptive treatment to the large teaching spaces was omitted as part of a cost cutting exercise exacerbated the situation, and led to a very unhappy set of staff. Anecdotally, the children did not seem as concerned by the noise but it was not a good design solution for the school as a whole. At Plymouth School of Creative Arts however the concept of team teaching was built into the philosophy of an entirely new school and the teachers were more receptive (Figs 12 and 13). They were able to practice teaching in larger and smaller integrated groups in an open plan space in nearby industrial building, and each class space was designed so

from left Fig 12/ Team teaching in open-plan areas was part of the philosophy behind the new Plymouth School of Creative Arts, wide corridors are used for display and performance, © Hufton + Crow; Fig 13/ The atria are used for dining as well as extending the teaching from glass-fronted classroom spaces; © Hufton + Crow.

that it could be subdivided naturally into three slightly separate areas using large-scale furniture. It was also acknowledged that the space could be more permanently divided if the team teaching didn't work. As for folding sliding screens, the anecdotal evidence is that they are rarely used and also the soundproofing has been known to degrade over time. Better perhaps to allow for subdivision to happen by relocating studwork walls which means working to a potential partition grid as with a flexible office floorplate.

Wider corridor spaces allowing for breakout from classrooms is more successful but does depend on a high level of trust between teachers and pupils, and in one instance where we fitted out such spaces with large semi enclosed areas teachers were concerned about some children behaving inappropriately in spaces where they could not be overseen so the furnishings were removed. Shared teaching areas do need some form of passive supervision, with staff workrooms looking onto

them, or glazed screens from classrooms enabling direct line of site, but in these circumstances, and with an atmosphere of trust set up between staff and pupils then they can enable a greater variety of teaching and learning spaces inhabited in different ways.

EXTERNAL SPACES

The wider landscape of the school provides not only for physical education and outdoor recreation but can contain a variety of teaching and learning spaces. The cut price solutions of tarmac and grass often provide a depressing setting for our buildings. Children need to be able to rush around and exercise and the ubiquitous multi-use games areas (MUGAs) offer the best opportunities for containing this activity. Providing a MUGA above the footprint of a sports hall means that both are the same functional size for the sports pitches they house.

In tight-knit urban sites we also end up using as much of the roof area as we can for recreation. Raised planters in those situations mean that the waterproofing of the roof deck remains simple with the planter resting above it. Planting beds can provide

seating along their edges and provide more protection for the plants (Fig 14). Trees can often make the biggest impact for minimum cost and maintenance but really need their roots in the ground.

Wherever opportunities exist in the site topography we try to introduce ampitheatrical spaces, simple and robust stepped seating which can allow for informal seating, for a gathering of students to be addressed by a teacher or even for small-scale performances. At Tor Bridge High school (Fig 15) stepped retaining walls and banks extend across the internal courtyard. At Islington Academy the stepped seating creates another type of performance space just outside the drama studio (Fig 16).

opposite Fig 14/ The grand scale of the steps at St Mary Magdalene Academy at Islington provides an informal and formal gathering space, © Hufton+Crow.

from left Fig 15/ Raised planters provide protection for landscaping on the roof terrace of Chelsea Academy, © Tim Crocker; Fig 16/ The central courtyard at Tor Bridge High school, © Craig Auckland Fotohaus.

THE ARCHITECTURE OF SCHOOLS

MATERIALITY

Fig 1/ Simple brickwork patterning adds an element of craftmanship and texture to simple areas of brickwork cladding at Tudor Grange Academy, © Craig Auckland Fotohaus.

Over the last ten years of experimentation in the architectural design of schools there has been a temptation to indulge in buildings that break the mould, designs that aspire to iconic status. The problem is that such an approach based on stylistic whims tends to produce an architecture whose appeal is short-lived. The century of state secondary education has produced a variety of 'styles' dominated by the first generation of buildings inspired by late Victorian gothic, and the second generation of post-war modernist buildings designed around a low-cost high speed production process.

Our own work has tended to avoid the overtly new and the clichéd, in favour of using traditional and robust materials which we hope will give our architecture a timeless quality. With a range of designers from different studios has come a range of materials and approaches but the more we build and the more we observe of the buildings we completed many years ago, the more we tend to rely on simple detailing and materials which are as maintenance free as possible, and which will weather elegantly and naturally.

EXTERNAL MATERIALS

So most of the buildings illustrated as exemplars in the third section of this book tend to be faced in brickwork. With this as a constraint in the choice of colour and texture, the patterning and pointing techniques become all important. There is a huge difference for instance between creating windows which are recessed a full brick into the wall rather than half a brick. The appearance of solidity gives the building a very different character for little extra cost and the recessed windows can help reduce solar gain. Solid brickwork columns can reinforce this robust appearance. We have also become interested in the relief patterning of brickwork, adding an element of craftsmanship to the facade (Fig 1), focused around key elevations and entrances. At Drapers' Academy the solid material becomes more of a folded curtain of brickwork above the entrance elevation and at Tudor Grange the texture builds to an intensity as the height of the wall rises towards the main street frontage.

We have built schools in render and enjoyed the potential this gives of brightly coloured surfaces but we have regretted the decision five years later with the potential for mould growth and damage to the surfaces close to the ground. Timber also tends to look great when first completed, and the natural warmth of the material is enjoyable. The natural weathering and colour fading can also work but generates a quality many find much less appealing and we would now be cautious about extensive use of treated softwood or larch. St Mary Magdalene Academy in Islington has managed to retain the quality of its facade partly because it was a higher quality timber (Fig 2) and partly because of the care that went into the detailing of joints and textures.

Occasionally we have used more industrial finishes: a high quality dark anodized aluminium cladding seemed appropriate for Aston Engineering Academy built on the edge of the Birmingham inner ringroad (p 103), and at Plymouth (p 139), where the desire for a bold architectural statement came from the client, and the form was generated by a very tight site, we chose a very low-cost red powder-coated steel sheeting to give the new school a strong identity in an edge of city context, where it also provides a 'gateway' to the city for those coming through the port. The design decision over the material quality here was heavily influence by cost, given the Free school budget, and we added a level of distinctiveness simply by the informal and irregular positioning of windows and the change in the rhythm of the folded joints. We live in hope that the colour will not fade and we protected the relatively thin sheets from damage by ensuring that the cladding is raised above an engineering brink plinth that runs right round the building.

Occasionally there is, we feel, an opportunity to be more celebratory in the colour and materiality of our school buildings. Highfields School in Blackpool for instance, seeks to be bold but not alien to its suburban context, drawing on the idea of the seaside architecture that the town is known for. Glazed tiles adorn the upper levels of the facade in a variety of blues and greens to create a strong, fluid and colourful identity to a building that is otherwise very restrained in its simple detailing and proportionality. Once again the slightly less robust tiling is restricted to the higher levels (pp 52–53) of the facade with the ground floor being clad in a blue-black engineering brick.

Fig 2/ The cantilevered slatted timber clad sports hall at St Mary Magdalene Academy, Islington, © Hufton+Crow.

STRUCTURAL SYSTEMS

If future flexibility is a critical issue then two-way spanning in situ concrete flat slab construction provides the optimal structural solution. The lack of downstand beams means that partitions can meet the underside of the slab anywhere, and providing you retain the additional floor to ceiling height it is easier to retrofit services. Spans of seven to nine metres each way suit both typical classroom dimensions whilst providing an efficient structural solution. For many schools this became our default structural solution. Columns can be either integrated and rectilinear or freestanding and circular. And a good quality exposed concrete soffit provides exposed thermal mass to reduce cooling loads.

Economies can often be made however by using a steel frame with precast concrete floors. Reduced cost means reduced flexibility and reduced quality of finish that comes with concrete to steel junctions. Even cheaper and you end up with the standard industrial floor using corrugated permanent profiled steel decking supporting a Cast concrete floor above. We adopted this deliberately for the Plymouth School of creative Arts (Fig 4) not simply because of the cost but also because of the industrial aesthetic which extends to the exposed pipework, sprinkler systems and electrical conduit all of which is exposed and therefore easy to access, but all of which can collect dust and, occasionally, projectiles.

Steel and concrete are the principle structural materials for most schools but William Perkins School in Ealing is a four-storey building where the contractor chose to use cross-laminated timber as the principle structural material. External and internal floor walls and roofs as well as staircases, are all constructed out of solid structural timber (Fig 5). Besides the considerable advantages of several weeks reduction in construction time because of prefabrication of all the loadbearing elements, it also meant that large areas of the timber structure could be exposed internally bringing the warmth and lightness of timber to a series of dramatic interior spaces. Timber has relatively low thermal capacity and the contractors were concerned about this leading to overheating, so phase change materials were built into areas of the classrooms where there were dropped ceilings to add to the apparent thermal mass. We have not yet been able to test its efficacy in use. An important additional benefit is that it was calculated that 3,200 tonnes of CO_2 were sequestered in the building, or saved by the omission of a steel and concrete frame. This is equivalent to approximately 30 years' worth of CO_2 produced through the operation of the building. As our buildings become more energy efficient, the embodied CO_2 statistics become even more significant.

previous page Fig 3/ Colourful glazed tiles at Highfields Humanities College Blackpool draws on the context of the seaside architecture, © Will Pryce.

above Fig 4/ The low-cost industrial structural and services left exposed give a robust background context to the Plymouth School of Creative Arts, © Hufton + Crow.

opposite Fig 5/ At William Perkins School in Ealing the entire structure is cross-laminated timber which left exposed in atria and circulation areas gives a natural warmth to the interior of the school, © Dominic Cole for Kier Construction.

FEILDEN CLEGG
BRADLEY STUDIOS
LEARNING FROM
SCHOOLS

THE
ENVIRONMENT
OF SCHOOLS

THE ENVIRONMENT OF SCHOOLS

LIGHT

ER Robson's 1874 book, *School Architecture* (see chapter 1), recommended a 1 to 5 ratio of window to floor area to ensure good quality natural light in a classroom. This was before the days of electrical light when classrooms also tended to have much taller ceiling heights, but it is interesting that this figure is very similar to the ratios that we use today, despite huge changes in the performance of glazing, as a starting point for getting the balance right between optimising natural daylighting and avoiding excessive solar gain. Another way of thinking about it is that our rule of thumb proportions for the ratio of transparent to opaque external wall surfaces should be around 30% and 40%.

Daylight of course is not just about lux levels. Exposure to daylight stimulates production of vitamin D and hormones such as melatonin and it also plays an important role in the circadian rhythm of the body as the quality of the light changes through the day. Many studies have explored daylight, emulating the natural light by using high temperature light fittings. Increasing the colour temperature in these studies was shown to improve visual acuity, memory recall, attendance, attainment and found to have a "relaxing effect"[1]. Beyond these outputs, daylight can be used to create feelings of openness, removing the dark corners that can be a source for antisocial behaviour within schools. An effective daylighting strategy therefore, not only improves the academic performance, but can improve the health and happiness of the students within a school.[2]

The importance of daylight in schools can be seen by the government's move from relatively simple daylight factors as design criteria (within Building Bulletin 90), to more complex Climate Based Daylight Modelling (CBDM). This explores the behaviour of the daylight over the whole year, not just under a uniform overcast sky, enabling robust predictions of daylight behaviour.

p 56 Paddington Academy, © Hufton + Crow.

opposite from left Figs 1 and 2/ Using the building to shade the windows. Overhangs and vertical exterior fins shade the windows at St Mary Magdalene and Paddington Academy, © Hufton + Crow; Figs 3 and 4/ Sunlight is reflected off interior surfaces to reach deep into the plan at William Perkins School and Drapers' Academy, © Jim Stephenson (middle right), © Timothy Soar (right).

above from left Fig 5/ Photovoltaic cells encapsulated in the rooflight at St Mary Magdalene Academy, Islington, provide shading and instructive evidence of the way light can be transformed into electricity, © Hufton + Crow; Figs 6 and 7/ Too much sunlight can be a problem in classroom areas but brings delight to circulation spaces at Drapers' Academy and Paddington Academy, © Timothy Soar (middle), © Hufton + Crow (right).

Bringing daylight into a school is not as simple as providing glazed areas: to create truly day-lit spaces while avoiding excessive solar gains and glare, daylighting can be difficult to manage. Schools have increasing ICT and high densities of occupants, so reducing glare and external gains is important to protect the other aspects of the school environment. The most effective way of controlling the daylight within the spaces is to effectively block the direct sunlight from reaching the working areas using external shading such as brise soleil, vertical fins or deep window reveals (Figs 1 and 2). Diffusing it once it is in the space by bouncing the light off internal surfaces can create more uniform natural lighting (Figs 3 and 4). At St Mary Magdalene in Islington we used photovoltaic cells to reduce solar gain in roof lights and generate electricity (Fig 5). These techniques rely on diffuse light to brighten the space, with the external shading allowing in atmospheric diffuse light, and internally reflected light naturally diffusing. With internal diffusers, attention must be paid to the overheating as the sun's energy is still reaching the space. Eliminating sunlight completely can result in spaces becoming deadened: the occasional shaft of direct sunlight can lift the spirit. But by allowing this to happen in less thermally sensitive spaces, such as atria or circulation areas, (Figs 6 and 7) the solar gains can be effectively separated from the teaching spaces. Understanding where the sunlight will be throughout the day is key to designing these internal and external shading and reflecting strategies, reducing the harmful glare and heating only where they present a problem.

Despite the research into the benefits of daylighting, a less tangible aspect is the connection to the outside that can be achieved with glazing. Within offices, research has shown that the availability of a view outside and the naturalness of the view (trees fields, etc) were related to increasing job satisfaction.[3,4] Actively creating view paths through the building, utilising internal glazing where necessary, can enable the external views to be brought within deep plan buildings, providing a distant but important connection to the outside world. We usually try to ensure we achieve open

views at the end of corridors even at the expense of the cost of additional corridor length simply to create a sense of connectivity with the external environment (Figs 8 and 9). Glazing between circulation spaces and classrooms is always a topic of great debate. On the one hand the glazing is costly and takes away useful wallspace: on the other it brightens and humanises circulation areas, gives the school a sense of communal identity and provides for passive communication between staff (Figs 10 and 11). Our default solution is to try to achieve about one or two metres length of full height acoustic glazing adjacent to each classroom door.

top Figs 8 and 9/ Views that end corridors make essential connections from the centre of the school to the outside world at Paddington Academy (left) and William Perkins School (right), © Hufton+Crow (left), © Jim Stephenson (right).

bottom Figs 10 and 11/ Glazed internal partitions activate and humanise circulation areas and give a school a sense of communal identity at The City Academy Bristol (left) and Brighton Aldridge Academy (right), © Morley Von Sternberg (left), © Tim Crocker (right).

As with all aspects of the built environment, a significant driver for occupant satisfaction is the amount of control the occupants have over their space. Incorporating simple blinds into the daylighting strategy (including rooflights) will enable the teaching staff to vary the light levels to suit their teaching activities, particularly important considering the increase in interactive white boards and projectors. To make the most of the potential saving from daylight it is necessary to control artificial lighting. Many of our schools incorporate daylight sensing and presence detection with the aim of reducing energy consumed by the lighting. While lighting can be a significant consumer of electricity, a manual override should still be incorporated, if for no other reason than enabling conscientious occupants to switch off the lights when they leave a space. To assist with the occupant ownership of the space, lighting should be zoned to promote daylight as the lead light source, with each lighting zone parallel to the daylighting source. This should be combined with an additional zone next to the teaching wall to enable the projectors to operate in a darker part of the class when necessary.

THE ENVIRONMENT OF SCHOOLS

HEAT

Our expectations of thermal comfort are continually rising and complaints over temperature conditions in schools tend to be around too much heat in summer rather than too little in winter. Perhaps the most tangible environmental aspect of any building is the air temperature. The very nature of schools makes ensuring the optimal temperature increasingly difficult, with high occupant densities, increasing ICT (and associated heat gains), and significantly improved building fabric all conducive to overheating. Thermal comfort in buildings is not a simple question of temperature, as it is often portrayed, but it is a multi-faceted and highly personal experience.

Much of the research is directly related to understanding what the thermal comfort boundaries are, rather than the impact on the educational outcomes. Wollner et al suggest that along with the air quality, temperature is often cited as one of the key environmental factors.[5] Their investigation into the literature found that poor thermal comfort could lead to poor student's behaviour. A study by the University of Southampton found that the students preferred a lower temperature than predicted by the thermal comfort models (between 20°C and 23°C), but stressed that their tolerance was closely related to outside temperature.[6] This link to the outside temperature is seen around the world, with Wong and Khoo similarly finding that there are links between expectations and comfort.[7]

One of the earliest design decisions related to the environmental services will be the main heat source for the school, which is often linked to the sustainability/renewable energy agenda for the site. The standard heat source is generally centralised gas-fired boilers, which are very robust heat sources and often the facilities team will be familiar with their operation. Where there is a renewable energy requirement, there will be a temptation to use biomass boilers as the lead source. Existing installations in schools, including our own, St Mary Magdalene and Brighton Aldridge Academy have been fraught with problems, nearly all relating to the lack of experience of these systems (including the design installation, or maintenance), but also the new supply chain requiring the school to source good quality wood chips. Without the quality fuel, and often there is a limited number of fuel sources in a given area, then the whole system can grind to a halt. It's for this reason that backup gas boilers are installed, bridging the additional periods of maintenance that are needed for biomass boilers, but regularly working as the lead heating source.

An alternative heat source is a heat pump, usually either air-source or ground-source, which can count as a low carbon technology, though a lot depends on how efficiently they run. Air-source heat pumps are not as efficient as ground-source heat pumps, typically producing 2.5 kW of heat for every 1 kW of electricity compared to up to 5 kW for ground source heat pumps. Heat pumps have a much better carbon performance if they are run off site generated electricity, but we have found that there is little space for an installation large enough to provide significant electrical input, though we have incorporated small PV installations for educational purposes (Figs 12 and 13). While not as efficient, they are much cheaper to install without the need for major groundworks.

Figs 12 and 13/ Photovoltaic panels are unlikely to provide more than a token contribution to a schools electrical demand but having them visible and making a measurable contribution is a worthwhile educational initiative, © Feilden Clegg Bradley Studios (top), © Ben Blossom (bottom).

Delivering heat into the various spaces of the school often requires a mixture of techniques, and space-specific solutions. Classrooms need a responsive system that gets to the correct temperature quickly, switches off when not needed, and is very quiet. Radiators fit the requirements, but at the expense of precious wall space. Where the wall space is too important, simple natural convectors can be incorporated into the perimeter furniture (science lab benches for example). Underfloor heating should be avoided for classrooms, with the long warm up time preventing effective control, and the rising heat releasing any trapped pollutants/allergens from the floor coverings to the detriment of the air quality.

In schools which need to have full mechanical ventilation, either through acoustic or air quality concerns, then the air system can be used to provide the heat; localised terminal units with heating coils tempering the supplied air. This strategy can reduce the amount of services physically within the classroom, simplifying the coordination and the classroom layouts. This simplification only works with intelligent zoning, where classrooms are bundled together to avoid an expensive terminal unit in each space. However, warm air systems are a comparatively inefficient heating system, needing air movement to carry the heat into the space, regardless of whether the space is occupied.

Fig 14/ The sports hall at St Mary Magdalene Academy: Air is delivered through vents at above head height in the walls and extracted at high level, © Hufton+Crow.

Larger open areas can prove difficult to heat, particularly where there are high ceilings such as in sports or assembly halls. Getting the warmth to the occupants generally requires the use of the only nearby surface to many of the occupants: the floor. Underfloor heating works very well, but needs to be separated out from the rest of the more conventional heating system to allow the longer warm up period for underfloor heating. Where the space is used more transiently, such as with sports halls we have successfully used more responsive, systems such as a warm air system (supplied at low level) (Fig 14) or radiant panels at ceiling level.

As with any of the M&E equipment in a school, the control method holds the key to creating the best environment possible in an efficient way. Central heating is common in homes and so the users have a familiarity with their systems, making controlling radiators with simple thermostatic radiator valves (TRV) a good choice. With all TRV valves, there is debate about whether to have them locked to a certain setting or allow the occupants to control them. This is very much for the school leadership to decide, but this is down to trust of the occupants and the facilities management style. If the facilities team are able to correct the TRVs regularly or educate the users on proper use, then adjustable TRVs are the perfect solution, giving the occupants control and the satisfaction that brings with it.

Connecting spaces together can complicate controls and needs to be done very carefully, zoning by the end use and orientation. An east-facing room may not need heating while a nearby north-facing room may, purely through the difference in solar gain. Using layers of controls can help with this, each space using a local TRV, but with the whole teaching zones controlled by a central timeclock. This central control can be used to heat only the areas that need heating during out-of-hours use, reducing the energy required.

Whereas heating in schools is largely straightforward, and responsible for a reducing percentage of carbon emissions overheating is a much more complex issue. Greater air-tightness and improved insulation are holding in the heat much more efficiently, to the extent that some spaces can be largely heated passively from occupants and equipment. During summer this positive attribute can be a huge hindrance, particularly as temperatures continue to rise due to climate change.

Our post-occupancy evaluations consistently show much more electrical use for ICT systems than anticipated, and whilst there are signs that there is more interest in efficiency of equipment than there was ten years ago, there is also a demand for more computer power. Reducing solar gains is also essential, orientating the building to reduce the direct summer sun, but allowing the sun during the dark winter months. Even with optimal orientation, the school will still need additional help dispersing the internal gains to prevent overheating. Ventilation becomes the most sustainable method to cool the building, using the generally much cooler external air to remove the heat in the spaces. This is closely related to the ventilation strategy and the same principals underpin the design (ensuring the whole space has air movement, using the natural buoyancy or wind pressure to drive the air). Where necessary, mechanical ventilation can be used to provide cooled air by coupling the air supply to relatively constant ground temperature, a labyrinth system (as we did at Aston Engineering Academy) or earth tubes (at the City Academy Bristol).

Combining exposed thermal mass and night ventilation can be a good way of peak-lopping: reducing the highs and lows throughout the day. To get the night ventilation strategy to work with natural ventilation systems there is a temptation to use automated window openers, but we have found this provides one more level of complexity which has the opportunity to go wrong! This should be resisted in preference for manual openings where possible. There is a lot to be said for a Caretaker or Facilities Manager doing a regular walk around the building last thing at night and opening a few secure vents to prevent summertime overheating!.

THE ENVIRONMENT OF SCHOOLS

AIR

Looking at the design criteria of the first generation of state secondary schools a century ago it is evident that ventilation was of absolute importance, much more so than heating. Of course this was an era when the benefits of fresh air were associated with the avoidance of prevalent lung diseases, but one also suspects, in an era when some children were sewn into their clothes for winter, there was also a necessity to remove odours!

Within school buildings, ensuring the indoor air quality remains acceptable is a key challenge; the high densities of students often coupled with difficult site constraints regularly cause difficult design decisions. The most widely accepted measurement of indoor air quality is the CO_2 level within the space. CO_2 has typically been used as proxy for air 'freshness' and the link between increasing CO_2 levels and deteriorating health and cognitive performance is well documented in research. Studies by University of Exeter and UCL have both found high CO_2 levels in classrooms regularly in excess of the 1500 ppm, and even some levels higher than the detector could read (over 4000 ppm!).[8, 9] Within Building Bulletin 101 and other school air quality guidance (CIBSE Guide A, Priority School Building Programme Output Specification) ventilation rates for spaces are given per occupant, reflecting the use of ventilation to disperse emitted CO_2. However, while CO_2 is clearly important, fresh air is not limited to simply reducing CO_2, but includes a range of pollutants that are commonly overlooked such as ozone, NO_x, carbon monoxide, particulates volatile organic compounds (VOCs) and allergens. All of these have had a measured effect on the health of the occupants, from sick building syndrome to asthma.[10, 11]

External pollutants cannot all be controlled in the same way, but instead need an understanding of the site and the sources of pollution. Through knowing the predominant wind direction and the sources of the air pollution, the school fresh air supplies can be located in cleaner air. The landscape of the site can be manipulated using trees to slow the wind, reducing the pollutants that reach the school while making the site feel greener and potentially helping with solar shading. By placing the teaching spaces away from the sources of pollution (away from roads or rail lines for example) then the spaces could use natural ventilation rather than relying on mechanical ventilation.

Ambient noise levels often dictate that mechanical ventilation systems are necessary, and interestingly, one of the main drivers for this is the fear that students taking examinations might have reason to complain if noise levels are too high. By providing air quality indicators and openable windows within the spaces, the teachers and students can have an influence on their own environment, which has been repeatedly shown to improve occupant satisfaction over purely mechanically ventilated buildings.

With natural ventilation as the cheaper and lower energy option, the key to reducing CO_2 and pollutant levels is to get the air moving across the spaces, with distinct and separate supply/extract routes for the air. This can be achieved using cross-ventilation, potentially using stack effects in atria or using roof-mounted, wind-driven ventilators. Given the importance of ensuring the fresh air is as clean as possible (such as in a city

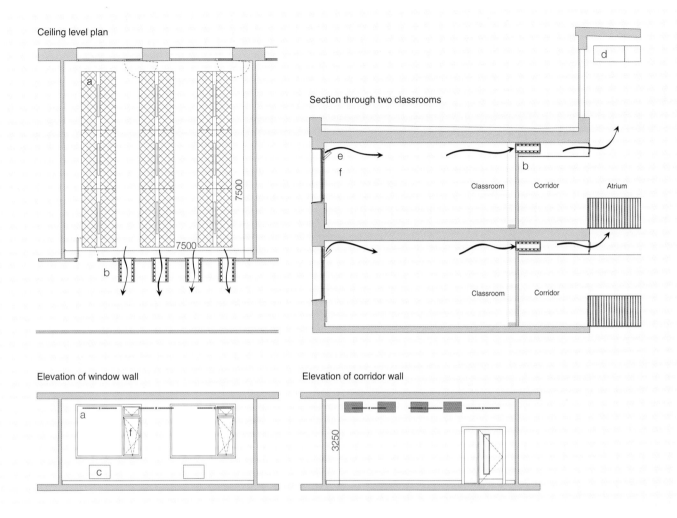

Ceiling level plan

Section through two classrooms

Classroom   Corridor   Atrium

Classroom   Corridor

Elevation of window wall

Elevation of corridor wall

Our latest schools use a simple, passive system, meeting the environmental needs of the students and school. From these schools we have created a typical classroom that is transferable to many different schools typologies. Using these typical classrooms we can develop some simple rules of thumb for glazing, vent areas and acoustic panels.

Acoustic panels: 35–40% of the floor area.
Glazing: 25–30% of external wall area.
External vent free area: 1.5–2.0% of the floor area.
Internal vent free area: minimum 50% of external vent-free area.

a.   Light fixtures incorporated into suspended acoustic rafts.
b.   Attenuated louvred airpaths at high-level into corridor ceiling.
c   Small radiators below windows.
d.   Natural ventilation airpath.
e.   High-level inward opening bottom hung panel for night cooling and interior fresh air.
f.   Low-level inward opening tilt/turn panel for purge ventilation.

centre) it can be prohibitively difficult to use a natural ventilation strategy, creating the need for a mechanical system. Using a mechanical system allows the fresh air supply to be located away from sources of pollutants, filtered to further improve noise and air quality, and can reliably provide the necessary fresh air rate to prevent build-up of CO_2. However, mechanical systems are not an answer to all problems: they bring increased maintenance and running costs, greater disconnect between occupant and building, and potentially complex control strategies; they can cause more problems than they solve. Without regular maintenance and cleaning, the mechanical system itself can be a source of pollutants. At Paddington the complex mechanical ventilation system which used an underfloor labyrinth for ground source cooling and delivered ducted fresh air to each classroom proved energy intensive simply because the filters were never properly maintained.

In Central London, the noise and pollution is a serious issue for all buildings, making natural ventilation difficult in new buildings. With Chelsea Academy (p 93) it was the fact that the school was on the Heathrow flight path that led to the decision to use mechanical ventilation to supply fresh air, filtering the air to remove particulates and keeping the ambient noise levels low to stop outside distractions. On such a tight site space is at a premium and the space used by the ductwork risers takes up potential teaching space. A simple solution was to use the three atria, removing the return ductwork and replacing with attenuated transfer grilles from the classrooms into the ceiling void, which then feed into the atria. This can then use the natural stack effect with the mechanical extract at the top of the atria to pull the air out of the classrooms. Nevertheless to give the occupants the ability to fine tune the control of their environment, each teaching space has an openable window.

At Aston University Engineering Academy, adjacent to an urban motorway, natural ventilation was always going to be difficult: noise and pollution preventing simple openings. However, the existence of an existing basement on the site led to the inclusion of a basement plant room with air taken through a labyrinth route of concrete block ducts before being introduced to spaces above. This tempers the air using the stable ground temperature, with the circuitous route increasing the time the air is exposed to the surrounding cool ground. We have been unable to monitor the efficiency of this system, but we are told the basement does remain cool through the summer months.

Our conclusions having completed a series of both naturally and mechanically ventilated schools, is to go for a natural ventilation system that uses cross-ventilation. The more stringent criteria of CIBSE's TM52 can be met through louvered, openable windows with sound attenuated airpaths into the circulation, helped by the stack effect of the tall atria to help pull the air through the classroom to dissipate the internal heat gains. By using louvered openings with solid shutters rather than opening lights there is no need for blackout blinds which would block the air flow, which is an increasing problem as teachers grapple with interactive white boards that are sensitive to light levels. All this ensures that the occupants can operate the ventilation in a familiar way; they don't need to think about the return air path, or moving the blinds, or noise from other spaces, they just open the louvered panel.

The environmental systems in our schools contribute to their carbon dioxide emissions. In 2008 the government set out a bold ambition to make all new schools zero carbon by 2016, and the Department for Education set up a Zero Carbon Task Force (ZCTF) to investigate how this could be achieved. Those of us who had been working in the field of low-energy design for many years were impressed with the ambition but sceptical of our ability, as designers, contractors and building users to deliver. Over the last ten years we have learned a lot more about energy consumption in our schools, and managed to achieve significant reductions in heating bills, but this has been countered by a dramatic increase in electricity consumption, predominantly IT based, which has meant that our ambition for zero carbon schools has been thwarted. The solution is possible but necessitates a redoubling of our efforts. It will require, as the ZCTF concluded, a halving of energy demand, a doubling of the efficiency of the equipment we use, and a halving of the carbon in the energy supply through using, centrally or locally, renewable energy sources. Each of these steps we can contemplate realistically, and together they could achieve the government's original target.

THE ENVIRONMENT OF SCHOOLS

SOUND

Some of the schools we have completed over the last year enforce a policy of silence while children are moving from classroom to classroom: others see the value of relaxation and communication between lessons. But at breaktimes schools are inherently noisy spaces, and acoustics have become a real area of concern over the last ten years as we have begun rebuilding our schools

There are three aspects of noise that need to be considered: airborne noise, impact noise and reverberation. Each is important and when not correct, can be detrimental to the learning environment. Such is the importance of the acoustic environment that it can easily lead the design, from the location and form of the building within the site, to the layout of the differing school spaces. The DfE and EFA use Building Bulletin 93 to set out guideline requirements, although they acknowledge that they are open to alternative performance standards.

There are many sources of airborne noise in the school environment; external to the school (planes, traffic, etc), external but within the school (playgrounds, sports fields), internal from other spaces (neighbouring spaces for example), and from within the space (air conditioning, projectors, etc). Impact noise also contributes to the ambient noise level, caused by the physical activity in neighbouring spaces, typically moving chairs or footsteps. High ambient noise levels have been shown to have negative effects on memory and performance in cognitive tests.[12] Not surprisingly, teachers struggle in noisy environments where the speech to noise ratio drops, with increased absenteeism due to sore throats in the short-term, and voice problems in later life for those consistently exposed to loud environments.[13]

Ensuring the acoustic environment remains suitable for learning, it is clearly necessary to keep the ambient noise level down. As with all environmental design, the best practice is to look at the passive methods of controlling sound, placing the sensitive areas away from sources of noise. Locating teaching spaces away from sources of noise is the simplest way to prevent high ambient noise levels, for example moving them away from nearby traffic. Brighton Aldridge Academy, for instance, sits above an arterial road and a key train line into Brighton, both of which create too much noise to allow natural ventilation on the facade overlooking the road/rail. Using the acoustics as a guide, a majority of the teaching spaces were placed on the opposite side of the building from the road, using the building as a natural sound break and allowing the rooms to be ventilated using openable windows. This principal can be applied just as readily internally, moving main circulation routes and canteens/communal areas away from teaching spaces. Segregating areas of high noise generation and low noise tolerance internally can significantly reduce both ambient noise and impact noise. By reducing the ambient noise levels it allows more freedom in the design, with natural ventilation strategies far easier to incorporate.

Reverberation of sounds within a space can be detrimental to the teaching environment, with long reverberation times causing difficulty hearing words. As the echos of words continue to reverberate, the vowels can overlap, drowning out the consonants and make speech intelligibility particularly poor, pushing the teacher into a spiral of gradually

increasing volume to drown out the echo. This has the same effect as high ambient noise levels, straining the voice of the teachers. Interestingly our post-occupancy research in open plan spaces leads us to believe that children are less concerned than their teachers are, but for many teachers high rise levels can be very stressful. The conventional rule of thumb suggests we need approximately 35–40% of floor area in acoustic absorption panel's in a typical classroom.

There are many different techniques for achieving this from less efficient perforated plasterboard to suspended acoustic rafts in which can be integrated with lighting, through to suspended vertical absorbers (Figs 15, 16, 17). We tend to avoid the more traditional approach of a full acoustical suspended ceiling because of the institutionality and banality it brings as well as the reduction in ceiling height and the isolation it provided from potentially useful thermal mass which can have a valuable role in reducing overheating. As with all environmental systems there is a synergy between the aspects of heat, light, air and sound absorption: all need to be considered holistically in school design (Fig 18).

1. Dunn, Rita, Jeffrey S Krimsky, John B Murray, and Peter J Quinn, "Light up Their Lives: A Review of Research on the Effects of Lighting on Children's Achievement and Behavior", *The Reading Teacher* 38 (9), 1985, pp 863–869. http://www.jstor.org/stable/20198961, accessed 29 September 2015.
2. Hathaway, WE,"Effects of School Lighting on Physical Development and School Performance", *The Journal of Educational Research*, 1995, pp 228–242.
3. Yildirim, Kemal, Aysu Akalin-Baskaya, and Mine Celebi, "The Effects of Window Proximity, Partition Height, and Gender on Perceptions of Open-Plan Offices", *Journal of Environmental Psychology*, 27 (2), 2007, 154–165.
4. Boubekri, M, and F Haghighat. "Windows and Environmental Satisfaction: A Survey Study of an Office Building", Indoor and Built Environment 2 (3), 1993, pp 164–172.
5. Pamela Woolner, Elaine Hall, Steve Higgins, Caroline McCaughey, Kate Wall, *A sound foundation? What we know about the impact of environments on learning and the implications for Building Schools for the Future*, Oxford Review of Education, 33:1, 2007, pp 47–70.
6. Despoina Teli, Mark F Jentsch, Patrick AB, James, *Naturally ventilated classrooms: An assessment of existing comfort models for predicting the thermal sensation and preference of primary school children, Energy and Buildings*, Volume 53, October 2012, pp 166–182.

7. Nyuk Hien Wong, Shan Shan Khoo, *Thermal comfort in classrooms in the tropics, Energy and Buildings*, Volume 35, Issue 4, May 2003, pp 337–351.
8. Coley, David A, Alexander Beisteiner, "Carbon Dioxide Levels and Ventilation Rates in Schools", *International Journal of Ventilation*, June 2002, Vol 1, No 1, pp 45–52.
9. Chatzidiakou, Evangenlia, Dejan Mumovic, Alex James Summerfield, and Hector Medina Altamirano, "Indoor Air Quality in London Schools. Part 1: 'performance in Use'", *Intelligent Buildings International*, 2004, pp 1–29.
10. Chatzidiakou, Lia, Dejan Mumovic, and Alex James Summerfield, "What Do We Know about Indoor Air Quality in School Classrooms? A Critical Review of the Literature", *Intelligent Buildings International*, 2002, pp 228–259.
11. Mi, Y-H, Norbäck, D, Tao, J, Mi, Y-L. and Ferm, M, "Current asthma and respiratory symptoms among pupils in Shanghai, China: influence of building ventilation, nitrogen dioxide, ozone, and formaldehyde in classrooms", *Indoor Air*, 16, 2006, pp 454–464.
12. Shield, B, and J Dockrell. "The Effects of Noise on Children at School: A Review", *Building Acoustics 10*, 2, 2003, pp 97–116.
13. Picard, M, and JS Bradley, "Revisiting Speech Interference in Classrooms", *International Journal of Audiology*, 40 (5), 2001, pp 221–224. http://informahealthcare.com.libproxy.ucl.ac.uk/doi/abs/10.3109/00206090109073117, accessed 29 September 2015.

above Brighton Aldridge Community Academy © Richard Chivers; Paddington Academy © Hufton + Crow; Paddington Academy © Hufton + Crow.

opposite Drapers' Academy © Timothy Soar.

overleaf Samworth Enterprise Academy, © Martine Hamilton Knight.

FEILDEN CLEGG BRADLEY STUDIOS LEARNING FROM SCHOOLS

EXEMPLAR SCHOOLS

NORTHAMPTON ACADEMY

CONSTRUCTION VALUE/ £19.75 million
COMPLETION/ December 2005

SPONSORS/ United Learning Trust and DCSF
CONTRACTOR/ Miller Construction
STRUCTURAL ENGINEER/ Buro Happold
M&E ENGINEER/ Buro Happold
COST CONSULTANT/ C M Parker Browne
LANDSCAPE CONSULTANTS/ Plincke Landscape

PHOTOGRAPHY/ © Peter Cook, © Amos Goldreich

NO OF PUPILS/ 1,420
AGE RANGE/ 11–18
AREA/ 12,480 sqm (gross area)
SPECIALISM/ Sport, business and enterprise

AWARDS/ 2007 Civic Trust Education Award,
2006 RIBA Award

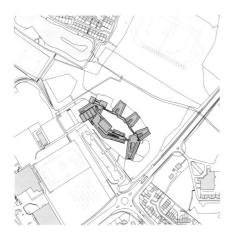

Northampton academy is one of our most successful courtyard schools. The site is on the edge of the city overlooking natural landscape; our aim was to create a visually permeable environment with views out from a central courtyard space. The brief from the United Learning Trust and the local authority was to deliver an extended school agenda providing both curricular and extracurricular facilities for pupils and the wider community.

Linked pavilions, each providing for a specific faculty area, follow a subtle non-orthogonal geometry around a sloping central courtyard, providing a social focus for the internal school community. The interaction of primary spaces, circulatory routes and views out to the surrounding landscape across changing levels, creates a stimulating and dynamic character to the heart of the school. A key feature of the organisation of the school is the enclosed circulation route at first floor level which forms a cloistered walkway at ground floor. The upper floor corridors are wide enough to provide breakout teaching spaces from the faculty pavilions.

While each faculty has its own distinct character, three of the four blocks have similar forms and plan arrangements with perimeter rooms around a triangular shaped double-height top-lit circulation area, designed to allow for flexibility in classroom use. The varied range of functions clustered in the fourth segment of the building lead to more varied architectural forms, creating a public face to the academy.

The entrance to the new building is framed by a double-height canopy that sits between a large volume of the sports hall and the glazed facade of the learning centre, providing an explicit link between the school and its 'external' community. The dining area which is located close to the communal school spaces can spill out onto the south-facing side of the courtyard.

The landscape design was given high importance due to both the existing ecological significance of adjacent sites and its potential contribution to the learning process. Teaching gardens are located between each faculty and given direct access from ground floor classrooms with a dedicated science pond area adjacent to the science faculty.

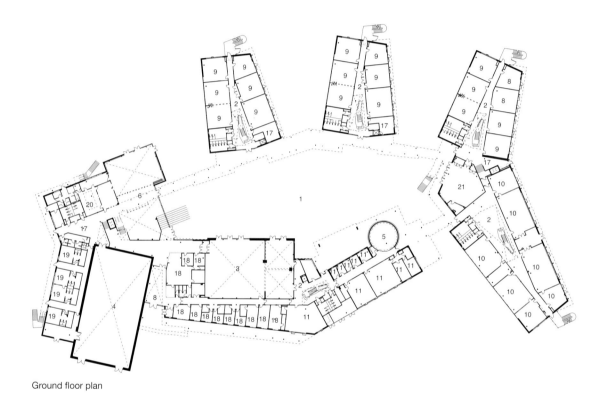

Ground floor plan

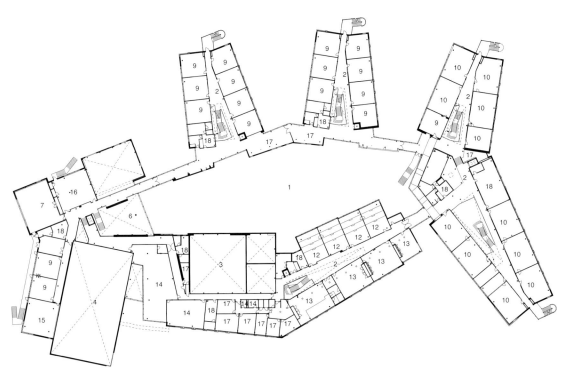

First floor plan

16. Sixth form room
17. Small group room/area
18. Staff/Administration office
19. Changing room

20. Kitchen
21. Professional development centre

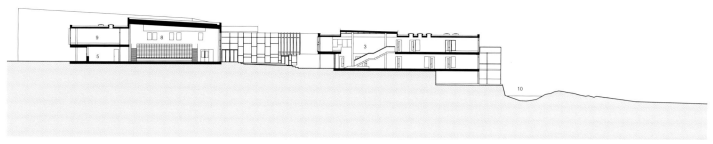

Section A

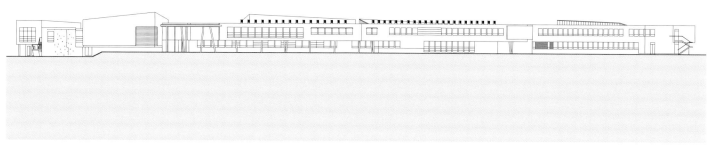

Elevation B

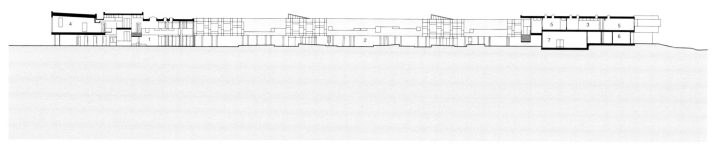

Section C

key 1. Dining hub   6. Science/DT teaching room
     2. Courtyard   7. Professional development centre
     3. Faculty hub   8. Assembly hall
     4. Dance studio   9. Library
     5. Staff/Administration office   10. SUDS — Sustainable urban drainage system

ST MARY MAGDALENE ACADEMY

CONSTRUCTION VALUE/ £27.7 million
COMPLETION/ Phase 1 September 2007 and
Phase 2 January 2009

SPONSORS/ London Diocesan Board for Schools
in conjunction with DCSF
PROJECT MANAGER/ EC Harris
CONTRACTOR/ Mace Plus
STRUCTURAL ENGINEER/ Buro Happold
M&E ENGINEER/ Buro Happold
COST CONSULTANT/ Davis Langdon
LANDSCAPE CONSULTANTS/ Churchman
Landscape Architects

PHOTOGRAPHY/ © Hufton + Crow

NO OF PUPILS/ Early Years Centre (53), Primary
(210), Secondary (900), Sixth Form (250), Total
(plus early years) 1,360
AGE RANGE/ Early Years Centre (6 months–
4 years old), Primary (4–11), Secondary (11–18),
Sixth Form (16–18)
AREA/ 11,278 sqm (gross area)
SPECIALISM/ Humanities and global citizenship
AWARDS/ 2009 RIBA National Award, 2009 RIBA
Stirling Prize: Longlist

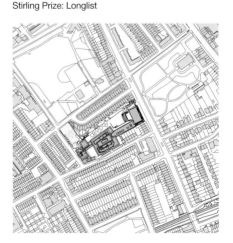

St Mary Magdalene Academy is an 'all-through' school in Islington offering continuity of education provision from reception to sixth form, with an integrated early years centre. Bounded by three streets, backing on to a Victorian terrace and fronting the civic space of St Mary Magdalene Church and gardens, the building footprint was pushed to the boundaries of the site, in order to maximise the area of outdoor space, whilst respecting the varying scale of the surrounding buildings and the privacy of residential neighbours. Considerations of orientation, daylighting, overshadowing, site acoustics and ecology all influenced the site planning.

The site's topography was exploited through the section allowing the early years, primary and secondary departments to each have independent entrances and designated external spaces, accessed from different levels on different streets. As a result, each of the three parts of the school has its own physical and architectural identity, even though the buildings are connected and they all benefit from a shared culture and ethos. Roofs were designed as usable areas, maximising their potential for ecological, social, educational and sports use, and for siting renewable energy technologies.

The ground floor of the school provides the major shared facilities for use by all age groups and the community, with the assembly spaces located off the main entrance to provide a civic entrance frontage topped by the rooftop MUGA. This large volume is clad in sharply detailed hardwood, subtly depicting the Christian sign of the fish across its entire facade, only visible when the sun casts shadows on the stepped and routed timber sections.

Echoing its larger scale neighbour, the primary hall is similarly clad in timber, marking out the more public facilities of the school as distinct from the stack-bonded brick tiles of the rest. Daylight is optimised in the teaching spaces with full-width glazing to all classrooms, providing single-sided natural ventilation. Laminated timber mullions add quality and richness to the interiors when seen against the marble-like quality of the concrete columns.

Internally the elongated plan of the secondary school is countered by the four-storey high 'forum'—the central focus of the school—with the elevated learning resource centre, again clad in timber, at its centre. The forum provides the dining area as well as a space that is large enough for the entire school community to assemble.

First floor plan

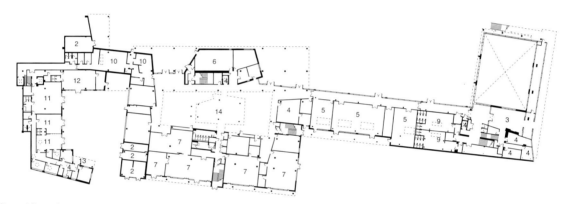

Ground floor plan

Basement floor plan

<u>key</u>

1. Multi-purpose hall	6. Lecture theatre	11. Nursery classrooms	16. Learning resource centre
2. Plant	7. Design & Technology	12. Reception classroom	17. Staff room
3. Main entrance	8. Headteacher's office	13. Nursery school entrance and reception	18. Primary school classroom
4. Administration	9. Changing rooms	14. Dining	19. Primary school hall
5. Art classrooms	10. Kitchens	15. Classroom	20. Primary school terrace

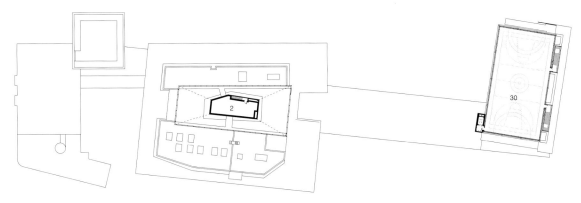

Fourth floor plan

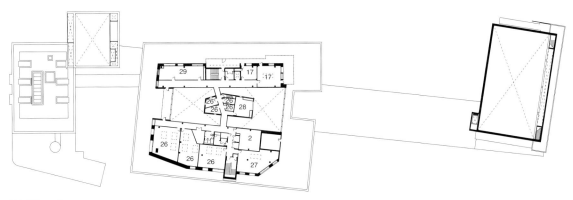

Third floor plan

Second floor plan

21. Sports hall
22. Gym
23. Primary school library
24. Primary school entrance
25. Science room

26. Music room
27. Post-16 social room
28. Prayer room
29. Media classroom
30. Multi-use games area

0   25m

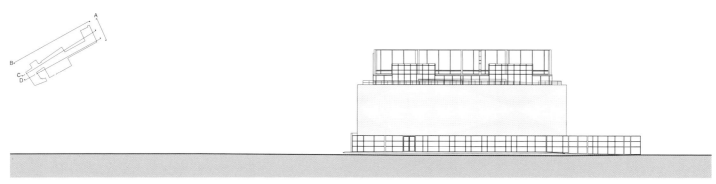

Elevation A

Elevation B

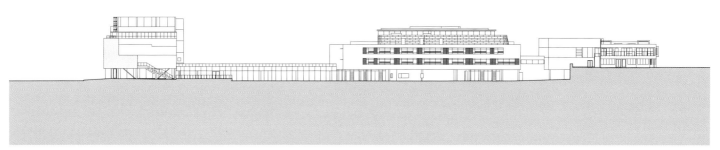

Section C

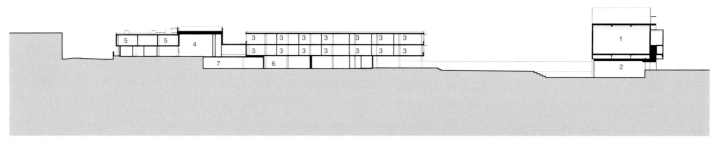

Section D

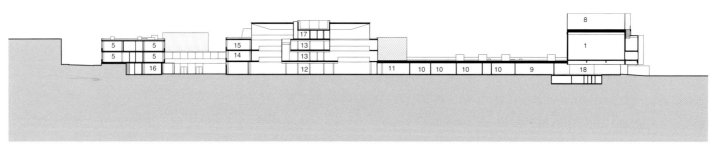

key					
1.	Sports hall	6.	Lecture theatre	11.	Administration
2.	Multi-purpose hall	7.	Kitchen	12.	Dining
3.	Classroom	8.	Multi-use games area	13.	Learning resource centre
4.	Primary school hall	9.	Changing rooms	14.	Multi-learning classroom
5.	Primary school classroom	10.	Art classroom	15.	Laboratory

16.	Nursery classroom
17.	Music practice room
18.	Main entrance

CHELSEA
ACADEMY

CONSTRUCTION VALUE/ £30 million
COMPLETION/ September 2010

SPONSORS/ RBKC (Royal Borough of Kensington
and Chelsea) and LDBS (London Diocesan Board
for Schools)
CONTRACTOR/ Wates Construction
**ORIGINATING DESIGN STRUCTURAL
ENGINEER/** Price & Myers
ORIGINATING DESIGN M&E ENGINEER/
Fulcrum Consulting
COST CONSULTANT/ Davis Langdon LLP
LANDSCAPE CONSULTANTS/ Churchman
Landscape Architects

PHOTOGRAPHY/ © Tim Crocker

NO OF PUPILS/ 162–180 in each year
AGE RANGE/ 11–18
AREA/ 11,000 sqm (gross area)
SPECIALISM/ Science
AWARDS/ 2012 Civic Trust Award: Commendation,
2011 Building Award Public Building of the Year

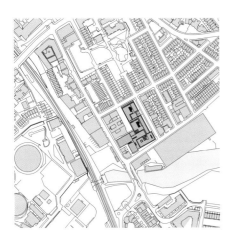

Chelsea Academy is a new type of high density urban school. Sponsored by the London Diocesan Board for Schools and The Royal Borough of Kensington and Chelsea, it is situated on a very constrained site in Lots Road, opposite a redundant power station. It is one of the smallest and most constrained sites we have been given to build on, with the nearby residential neighbourhoods resulting in restrictions to the height of the building on three sides. The minimal site area meant that virtually all the site was built on, that the building line is generally the back of pavement, and play areas were located on roofs. Height constraints necessitated digging down into a basement area for the larger sports and assembly hall spaces.

The Academy specialises in the sciences and is assisted by the development of close links with the museums, universities and similar institutions that are located in the Royal Borough. The science laboratories are located in a five-storey block which also contains the library and main public entrance facing the old power station. A secondary entrance spills out onto a pedestrianised mews street at the back of the building.

Typologically the school is organised around three interconnected buildings each organised around a central lightwell and each having a specific curricular significance. The buildings are linked together at ground floor level via a wide internal 'street' running north to south, but there are also links at rooftop levels.

The new Academy uses simple and appropriate environmental principals including optimising natural light, using exposed concrete soffits as thermal mass and renewable energy by using a bore hole that provides more than 10% of the energy demand on site. Because the school sits on the London Heathrow flightpath it had to be mechanically ventilated, but there are opening windows in each classroom to provide some localised climate control.

The generous windows provide good quality daylight and enable the users to be aware of the surrounding urban context from within the building and, consequently, Chelsea Academy feels more expansive and has strong connections with its neighbourhood. The external terraces are important as they not only provide areas for socialising but break down the potential large mass of the building into smaller fragments and a built form that does not need to compete with the power station, but complement the surrounding buildings as an ensemble.

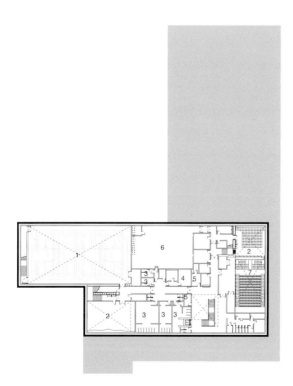

Lower ground floor plan

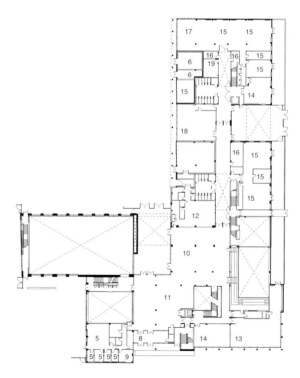

Ground floor plan

key

1. Sports hall
2. Studio
3. Changing
4. Therapy room

5. Office
6. Plant
7. Main hall
8. Reception

9. Principal
10. Restaurant
11. Sixth form cafe
12. Kitchen

13. Library
14. Business/IT classroom
15. Design & Technology
16. Staff office/Work room/Meeting room

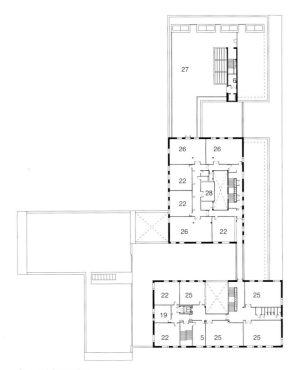

Second floor plan

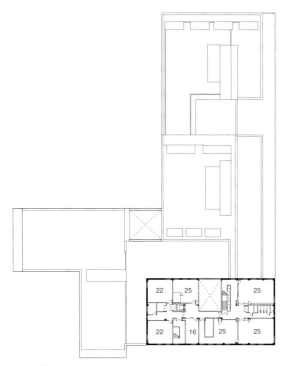

Fourth floor plan

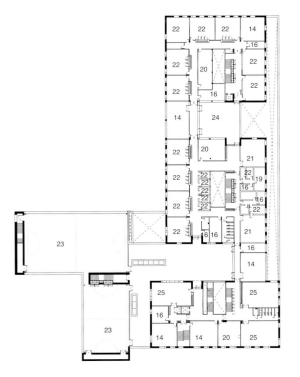

First floor plan

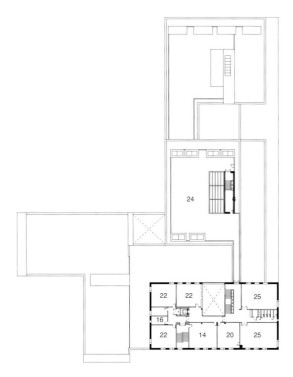

Third floor plan

17. Graphics
18. Food technology
19. Teaching support
20. Seminar/Open teaching space

21. Music rooms
22. General teaching
23. Multi-use games area/Training
24. External teaching space

25. Science room/Laboratory
26. Art room
27. Art external space
28. Prayer room

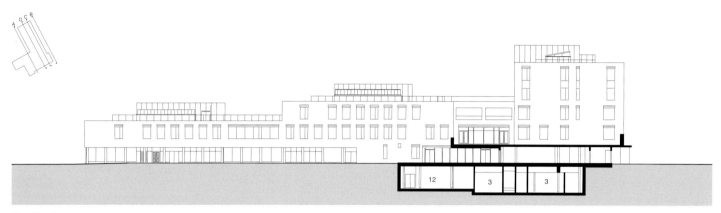

Elevation A

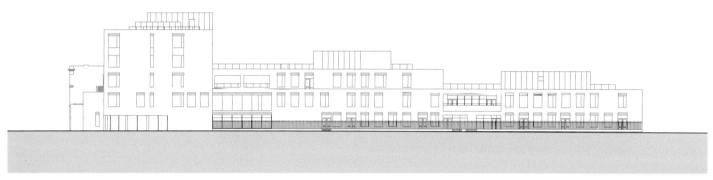

Elevation B

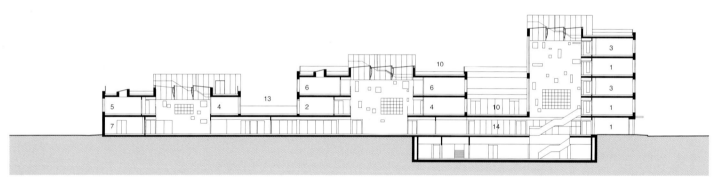

Section C

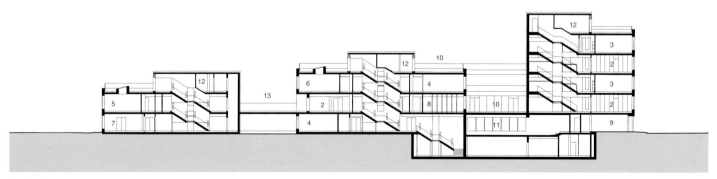

Section D

key	1. Business/IT classroom	5. General teaching	9. Library	13. External teaching space
	2. Seminar/Open teaching space	6. Art room	10. External social spaces	14. Restaurant
	3. Science laboratory	7. Design & Technology	11. Main hall	
	4. Staff Office/Work room/Meeting room	8. Toilets	12. Plant	

ASTON UNIVERSITY ENGINEERING ACADEMY

CONSTRUCTION VALUE/ £11 million
COMPLETION/ September 2012

SPONSOR/ Aston University
CONTRACTOR/ Lend Lease
STRUCTURAL AND CIVIL ENGINEER/ Cox
Turner Morse Limited
M&E AND ACOUSTIC ENGINEER/ Cundall
COST CONSULTANT/ Lend lease
LANDSCAPE ARCHITECT/ Planit

PHOTOGRAPHY/ © Steve Mayes Photography

NO OF PUPILS/ 120 year 10 and 180 year 12
AGE RANGE/ 14–19
AREA/ 8,304 sqm (gross area), 6,293 sqm (net area)
SPECIALISM/ Engineering
AWARDS/ 2013 RIBA Regional Award

Aston University Engineering Academy provides a new type of specialist learning environment for 14–19 year olds in the heart of Birmingham city centre, situated on a recently vacated inner city industrial site. The 600 student Academy has close links with the nearby university and other education and industrial partners; and is intended to be a show case for engineering skills.

The project brings together facilities that meet the ethos, vision and aspirations of the sponsor, Aston University, in a single, new 'superblock' building. The Academy has an engineering specialism and offers significant opportunities for students, staff, employers, members of the university and the wider community, as well as specialised education provision for a wide catchment area across the Midlands.

The new building is a low-cost compact form arranged around a central hall and adjacent atrium that in turn links to four 'home bases', the learning resource centre and dining spaces. The massing and organisational principles of the Academy have led to a building that is predominantly three-storeys; however this rises to four storeys along the adjacent inner city ring road due to the sloping nature of the site. This additional height helps to give the school a significant presence along the main road and affords the opportunity to express the engineering functions of the building via large shop front windows facing onto the dual carriageway beyond. An existing basement was retained and used both as a plant area and a thermal storage space to reduce the cooling requirement of the building which is mechanically ventilated because of the acoustical impact of the adjacent road.

The building is constructed from locally sourced dark blue-black engineering bricks and black anodised extruded aluminium cladding. Inside the finishes are white and grey but there are occasional accents of colour. One of these is at the main entrance (at both ground and first floor level) at the southwest corner of the site which reinforces a pedestrian link back across the canal to the wider Aston University campus.

0   50m

Ground floor plan

Second floor plan

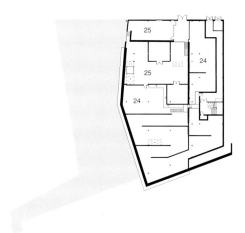

Basement floor plan

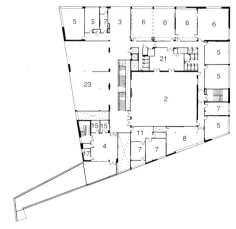

First floor plan

key				
1.	Refectory	8.	Gym	15.	Meeting room	22.	Specialist classroom
2.	Main hall	9.	IT classroom	16.	Student reception	23.	Library
3.	Homebase	10.	Specialist engineering classroom	17.	Medical suite	24.	Thermal labyrinth
4.	Reception	11.	Art classroom	18.	Terrace	25.	Plant
5.	Standard classroom	12.	Facilities offices	19.	Sixth form space		
6.	Science classroom	13.	Kitchen	20.	Music rooms		
7.	Office	14.	Archive	21.	Store		

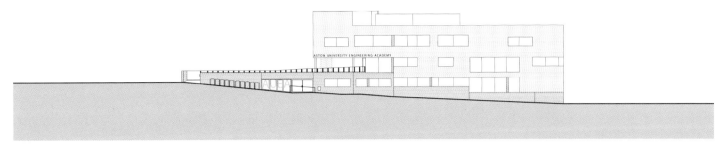

Elevation A

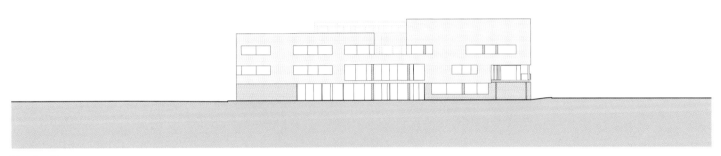

Elevation B

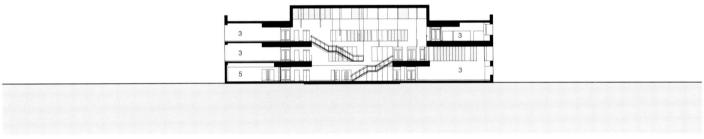

Section C

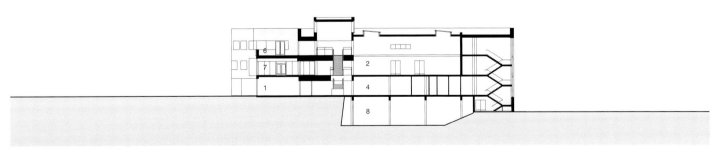

Section D

key			
1.	Refectory	5.	Specialist engineering classroom
2.	Main hall	6.	Terrace
3.	Homebase	7.	Library
4.	IT classroom	8.	Thermal labyrinth

HIGHFIELDS HUMANITIES COLLEGE

CONSTRUCTION VALUE/ £23 million
COMPLETION/ January 2013

CLIENT/ Blackpool Local Education Partnership
(a public private partnership between Blackpool
Council, The Eric Wright Group and Northgate
Management Services)
CONTRACTOR/ Eric Wright Construction
STRUCTURAL ENGINEER/ Booth King
Partnership Ltd
M&E ENGINEER/ RPS Group
COST CONSULTANT/ Eric Wright Construction
LANDSCAPE ARCHITECT/ Plincke Landscape

PHOTOGRAPHY/ © Will Pryce

NO OF PUPILS/ 1,200
AGE RANGE/ 11–16
AREA/ 12,482 sqm (gross area)
SPECIALISM/ Humanities

Highfield Humanities College is a state secondary school of 1,200 pupils between the ages of 11 and 16. It forms part of Blackpool's Building Schools for the Future (BSF) programme and has replaced what was a dilapidated existing college building.

The brief from the local authority was to replace run-down buildings with flexible, bright and open spaces. These had to be versatile enough to adapt to the changing needs of education and appealing enough to engender pride among the local community. The new design optimises this connectivity with large windows offering panoramic views to the surrounding community and local landscape. It has recreated the school as a single entity, focused around one main space. This "great room" is the heart of the school shared by the community of staff and pupils. Public, privileged and private spaces are openly connected to this central space and accessed directly from it.

The school's specialist focus on humanitarian issues and interpersonal relations has been strongly reflected in the design concept for Highfield. Learning environments, pastoral and social spaces are located within the same space and are visibly connected to each other. The design philosophy evolved from the whole school model that we developed in conjunction with the Highfield contractor, school and the local authority. The concept was of a building that personifies the relationship between individual aspiration and collective responsibility, and that the design of Highfield will encourage a stronger connection between the school and its neighbourhood.

The visual identity of the building draws on the wider architecture of Blackpool where the tower, casino and pleasure beach form the principal buildings of the town, rather than civic buildings or churches. The architectural design for Highfield seeks to be bold but not alien in its context and uses traditional materials while drawing on references from both seaside and domestic architecture. Glazed tiles adorn the facade in a variety of blues and greens to create a strong, fluid and colourful identity but one that is restrained and classic in its simple detail and proportion.

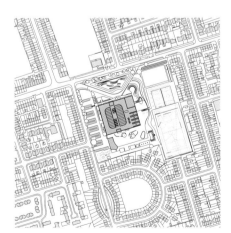

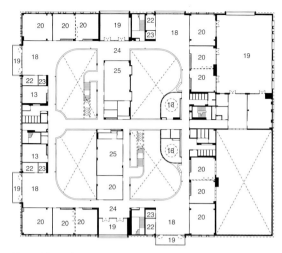

Second floor plan

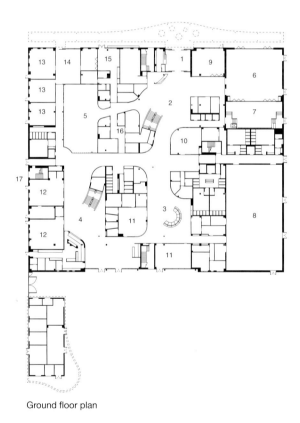

Ground floor plan

First floor plan

key					
1.	Main entrance	8.	Sports hall	15.	Learning support hub
2.	Welcome space	9.	Drama hub	16.	'Green House' – Pastoral care
3.	Informal performance	10.	Fitness suite	17.	Learning gardens
4.	Dining	11.	Music	18.	Inspiration hubs
5.	Library	12.	Technology	19.	Learning terraces
6.	Theatre/Gym	13.	Seminar rooms	20.	Classrooms
7.	Drama studio	14.	Vocational learning entrance	21.	Practical science

22.	Small groups
23.	One to one meeting rooms
24.	Informal learning pairing space
25.	Art classrooms

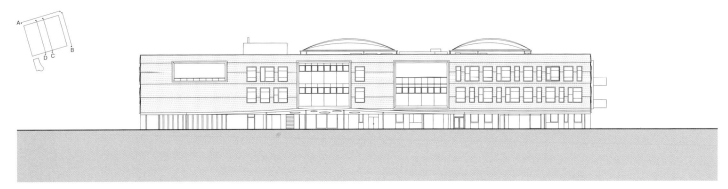

Elevation A

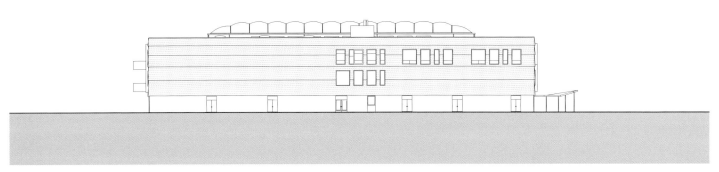

Elevation B

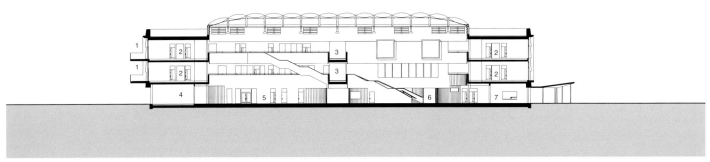

Section C

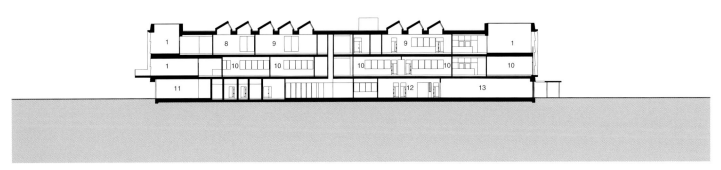

Section D

key

1. Learning terraces
2. Inspiration hubs
3. Bridge connections
4. Music hub

5. Informal performance
6. Welcome space
7. Main entrance
8. Classroom

9. Art classrooms
10. Practical science
11. Dining
12. 'Green House' — Pastoral care

13. Learning support hub

DRAPERS' ACADEMY

CONSTRUCTION VALUE/ £21.4 million
COMPLETION/ May 2012

SPONSORS/ The Drapers' Company and Queen Mary University
PROJECT MANAGER/ EC Harris
CONTRACTOR/ Kier Construction London
STRUCTURAL ENGINEER/ WSP UK
M&E ENGINEER/ WSP UK
COST CONSULTANT/ Kier Construction London
LANDSCAPE CONSULTANT/ EDCO Design London

PHOTOGRAPHY/ © Timothy Soar

NO OF PUPILS/ 1,100
AGE RANGE/ 11–18
AREA/ 10,692 sqm (gross), 10,600 sqm (net)
SPECIALISM/ Maths and science
AWARDS/ 2014 RIBA National Award, 2014 Civic Trust Award: Commendation

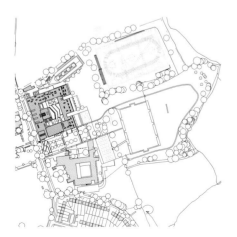

Drapers' Academy is sponsored by the Worshipful Company of Drapers and was opened by their patron, Her Majesty the Queen. It is a new building for a new educational institution replacing an existing secondary school on the edge of the post-war suburban development of Harold Hill. Dagnam Park, a grand country house, once occupied the site and looked out onto a Humphrey Repton landscape which still provides a setting for the school. The Academy has been designed to provide educational facilities for 900 pupils in years 7 to 11 and a 200 pupil sixth form. Its specialism in science and mathematics means it can benefit from connections with the staff and facilities of its sponsor Queen Mary University.

With a spectacular site on the edge of the green belt, the building and arrangement of the spaces aims to respond both to the natural topography that slopes towards the east and to the brief requirement for a variety of curriculum possibilities, whilst providing flexibility and adaptability for the future. Designed around a central courtyard, the school is organised around a progressive pedagogical learning journey anti-clockwise around the building

The building presents a three-storey facade to the community of Harold Hill with a textured 'curtain' of brickwork announcing the location of the main entrance. The structures reduce in height and then step down the hill to open the courtyard and upper floors to views out into the surrounding landscape. The site has influenced the final form of the building and the way it is enclosed by and encloses this landscape.

Taking cues from medieval cloisters and the sequences of rooms presented in English country houses, the architectural language of the building uses robust masonry detailing to create a clean crisp modern brick building. Solid and textured brickwork, deep window reveals with generous areas of glazing, and bronze louvred ventilator panels all help to generate a sense of purposeful solidity and provide a physical manifestation of the longevity of the Academy's educational intentions. Principle community spaces, as well as the major science demonstration areas are located along a linear internal street which then unfolds as a lower series of buildings around a stepped central courtyard.

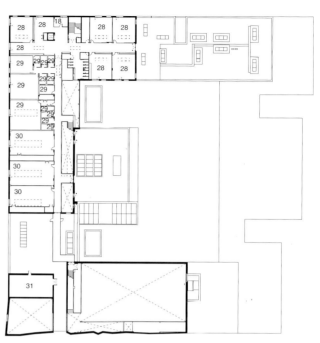

Second floor plan

Ground floor plan

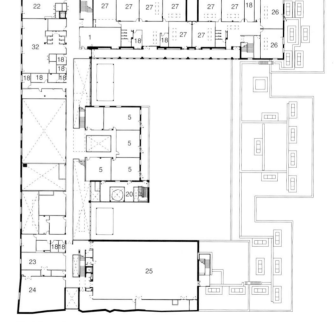

First floor plan

key							
1.	ICT classroom	9.	Learning Resource Centre	17.	Engineering	25.	Sports hall
2.	Maths classroom	10.	Hall	18.	Office	26.	MFL classroom
3.	Humanities classroom	11.	Cafe	19.	Kitchen	27.	English classroom
4.	Business classroom	12.	Main entrance	20.	Winter garden/Biodome	28.	Sixth form rooms
5.	Science laboratory/Studio	13.	Reception	21.	Dining	29.	Music rooms
6.	Food technology	14.	Changing room	22.	Textiles	30.	Art classroom
7.	Resistant materials	15.	3D theatre	23.	Gym	31.	Plant
8.	Drama studio/Stage	16.	Graphics	24.	Activity studio	32.	Staff room

0 ————————————— 25m

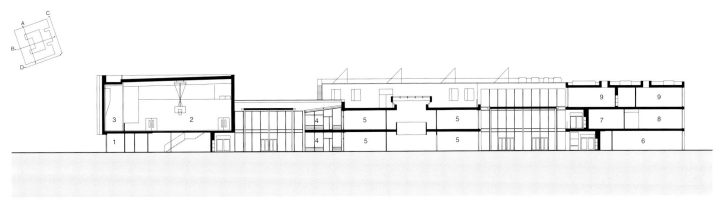

Section A

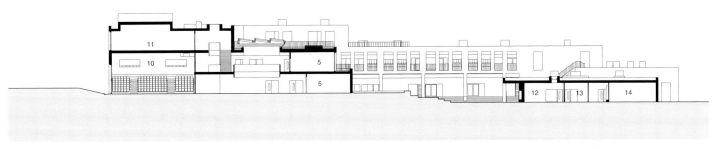

Section B

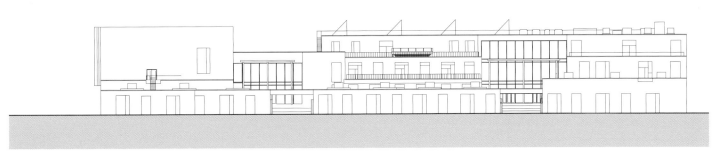

Elevation C

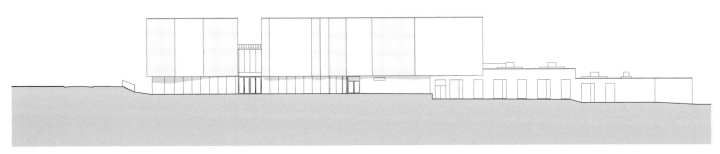

Elevation D

key
1. Main entrance
2. Sports hall
3. Climbing wall
4. Winter garden/Biodome
5. Science laboratory/Studio
6. Food technology
7. ICT room
8. English classroom
9. Sixth form classroom
10. Hall
11. Art classroom
12. 3D theatre
13. Office
14. Maths classroom

WILLIAM PERKIN
CHURCH OF ENGLAND
HIGH SCHOOL

CONSTRUCTION VALUE/ £18 million
COMPLETION/ Phase 1 August 2013 and Phase 2 February 2014

CLIENT/ Twyford Church of England Academies Trust, sponsored by London Diocesan Board for Schools
CONTRACTOR/ Kier
STRUCTURAL ENGINEER/ AECOM
CLT SUBCONTRACTOR/ KLHUK (and Ramboll as Structural Consultants to KLHUK)
M&E ENGINEERING/ KPE
COST CONSULTANT/ Kier also managed costs and budgets
LANDSCAPE ARCHITECT/ EDCO Design Limited

PHOTOGRAPHY/ © Jim Stephenson, © Dominic Cole for Kier Construction

NO OF PUPILS/ 1,200 pupils plus 250 sixth form and 12–36 Special Educational Needs pupils
AGE RANGE/ 11–18
AREA/ 11,279 sqm (gross), 10,947 sqm (net)
SPECIALISM/ Science and languages
AWARDS/ 2015 New London Architecture Awards: Education, 2015 RIBA Regional Award

The form of William Perkin Church of England High School synthesises a response to very specific contextual conditions with the client's education vision. The design brief spoke passionately of providing "an outstanding school which consciously serves, supports and involves the local community" and an environment that would be a "place of calm purposefulness". Inclusive design is embedded in our approach.

Within a suburban setting the site is heavily characterised by the presence of the A40 motorway to the south and a gracious line of poplar trees following this boundary. Planning constraints specifically restricted the footprint but not the height of the building. We responded by designing a building that forms an environmental shield to the harshness of the motorway whilst being outward-looking to its community.

These constraints guided us towards a simple, elegant concept where the school has two distinct parts—the rectangular 'bar' building, parallel to the A40, and the triangular 'apex', addressing the community. The two elements are connected by a street at ground floor, with an extended view along the line of poplars. Along the street, slots of light from above recreate the rhythm of dappled light from the trees beyond. The vertical bands of metal cladding, which articulate panels of flat and feathered brickwork along this elevation, continue the expression of the rhythm of the poplar trees to occupants of passing vehicles along the A40.

To meet a demanding programme the superstructure was designed in cross-laminated timber (CLT): 3800 m^3 of CLT and glulam frame was erected in 19 weeks, making William Perkin the largest timber structure in the UK. The exposed timber gives the heart of the school a distinctive warmth and character. Drama is brought to these spaces by four atria that offer views through the building, out to the sky, and across into different teaching areas.

The bar building houses the major communal and gathering spaces, most of which will also be used by the community. The laboratories are also located here, expressing the school's science specialism, as inspired by the nineteenth century chemist William Perkin.

The paradoxes, contrasts and juxtapositions within William Perkin Church of England High School increase the richness of the surroundings through variations in colour, texture, light and form, resulting in a place of 'calm purposefulness'.

Ground floor plan

key   1.   General teaching   5.   Kitchen   9.   Changing rooms   13.   Office
       2.   Music room   6.   Main hall   10.   Special education needs   14.   Entrance
       3.   Dining   7.   Plant room   11.   Autistic spectrum disorders   15.   Recording studio
       4.   Food technology   8.   Studio   12.   Calm room   16.   Learning resource centre

0   50m

Third floor plan

Second floor plan

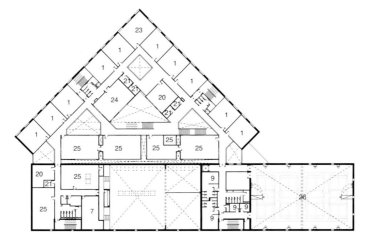

First floor plan

17. Book store	21. Senior management	25. Science rooms
18. Meeting room	22. Language laboratory	26. Sports hall
19. Reception	23. Seminar room	27. General teaching/Art
20. Staff work	24. IT/Webdesign/Graphics	28. Art barn

0   25m

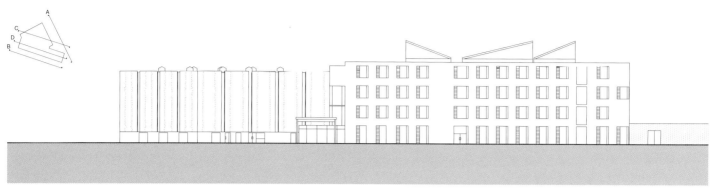

Elevation A

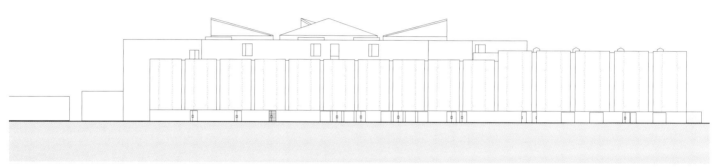

Elevation B

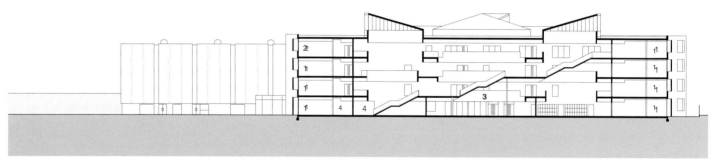

Section C

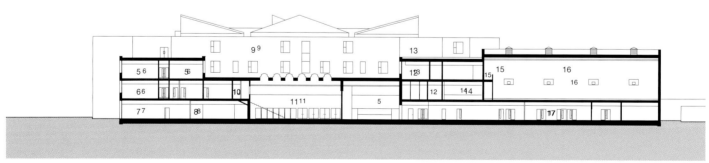

Section D

key 1. General teaching
     2. General teaching/Art
     3. Learning resource centre
     4. Reception
     5. Studio

     6. Science rooms
     7. Dining
     8. Kitchen
     9. Green roof
     10. Control room/Gallery

     11. Main hall
     12. Pupil changing
     13. Senior management
     14. PE store
     15. Gallery

     16. Sports hall
     17. Administration/SEN/ADL circulation

PLYMOUTH SCHOOL OF CREATIVE ARTS

CONSTRUCTION VALUE/ £9.5 million
COMPLETION/ March 2015

SPONSORS/ Plymouth College of Arts
CONTRACTOR/ Kier Construction
STRUCTURAL ENGINEER/ Jubb Consulting
M&E ENGINEER/ Aecom
COST CONSULTANT/ Gleeds
LANDSCAPE CONSULTANTS/ Rathbone
Partnership

PHOTOGRAPHY/ © Hufton + Crow

NO OF PUPILS/ 1,020
AGE RANGE/ 4–16
AREA/ 6,902 sqm (gross area)
SPECIALISM/ Creative arts

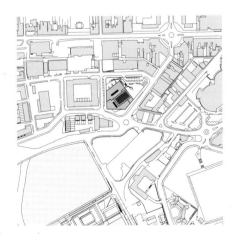

Affectionately known as the Red House, Plymouth School of Creative Arts is a 4 to 16 'all-through' free school sponsored by Plymouth College of Art. The school and college form a unique continuum of creative learning from nursery school to degree course and post graduate level. The school is a place for making things—making ideas, making technology, making art—for discovering how knowledge, values and language, identity or experience is made. It is a place of performance in both senses: performance as doing; performance as achievement; a place of creative learning in all subjects.

The building makes a bold statement. Its sculptural form is the first observable feature entering the city from the ferry port. Its urban character connects to the wider regeneration of the area where it is located and to the College of Art just the other side of the city centre.

The head teacher talks about the building as being a "provocation" for the education of the children. It embraces unconventional teaching methods founded in arts and studio culture. Internally three interlocking spaces create clarity, legibility and a unique teaching atmosphere, where knowledge and creativity can flow between teachers and peers. Large-scale classroom spaces are designed around the philosophy of a team teaching with three teachers and 75 children sharing sub-divisible spaces.

As an 'all-through' school the building has been carefully designed to ensure that there is a managed progression through the school creating rites of passage which culminates in the Phase 4 accommodation being located at the top of the school with direct access onto the second floor terrace. Similarly the opportunities for the school to bring the different ages together through the dining spaces and teaching spaces overcomes and addresses many of the issues that result from changing from primary to secondary school.

It is one of the lowest cost school buildings we have designed, with industrial finishes inside and out. The introduction of a dramatic glazed cut entrance space to the south provides transparency directly into the main entrance hall and dining space and has been referred to as the signature of the building. The informal composition of the windows and the colouring of the building clearly expresses that this is a creative building for the arts, along with integrating showcase windows into studio spaces to enable staff and pupils to display their creative outputs.

0   50m

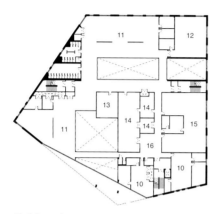

First floor plan

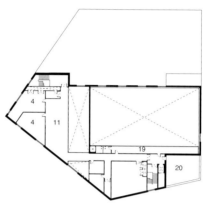

Third floor plan

Ground floor plan

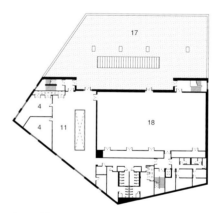

Second floor plan

key 1. Main entrance   6. Main hall   11. Class studio   16. Gallery
     2. Dining area and community space   7. Music/Activity/Drama studio   12. Presentation & Design   17. Terrace play area
     3. Culinary art   8. Recording studio   13. Textiles   18. Sports hall
     4. Classbase   9. Display of work   14. Make workshops   19. Viewing gallery
     5. Phase 1 and 2 entrance   10. Leadership & Resource   15. Science laboratories   20. Terrace

0   25m

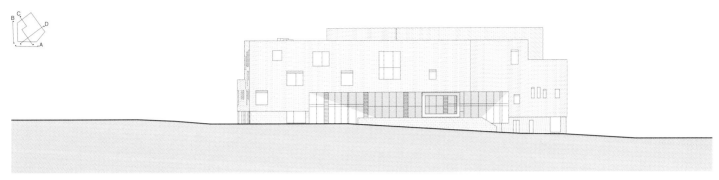

Elevation A

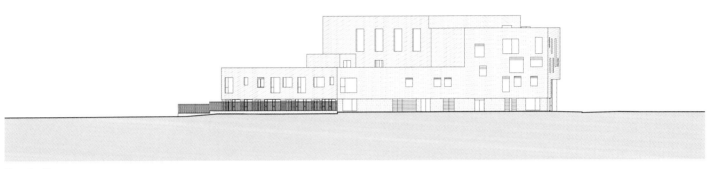

Elevation B

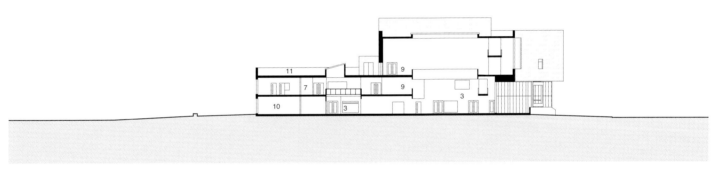

Section C

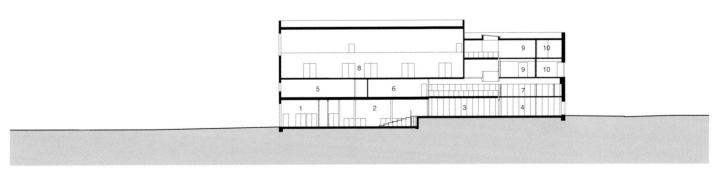

Section D

key
1. Activity studio
2. Main hall
3. Dining area and community space
4. Culinary arts
5. Science laboratory
6. Make workshop
7. Class studio
8. Sports hall
9. Open teaching
10. Classbase
11. Roof terrace play area

FEILDEN CLEGG
BRADLEY STUDIOS
LEARNING FROM
SCHOOLS

CONCLUSIONS

CONCLUSIONS

ATTAINMENT

JOE JACK WILLIAMS AND IAN TAYLOR

With the clear significance of schools within society, there has been considerable investment in recent years in school infrastructure, attempting to overcome years of under-investment. The most ambitious of these building programmes was the Building Schools for Future programme (BSF), which set out to improve all secondary schools in England. This programme ended in 2010, but not before over 550 schools had been significantly improved (over 80% renovation) or completely rebuilt. The development

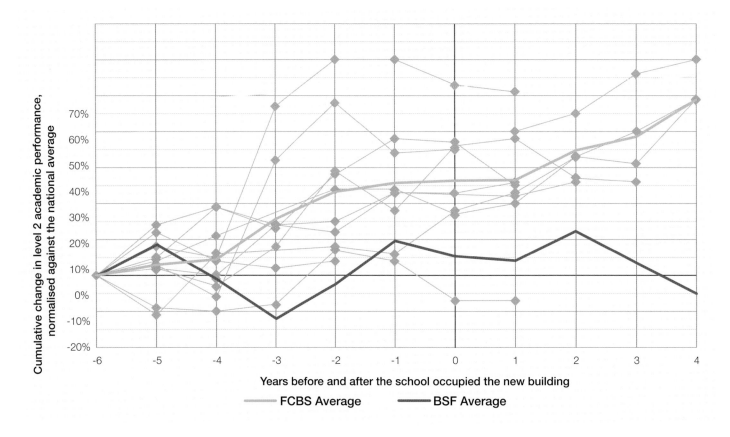

Fig 1 Graph showing the progress of FCBS schools compared to the BSF mean from a sample of 75 schools. Each of the fine lines represents the attainment of one FCBS designed school, which have not been labelled to keep their anonymity. This shows the cumulative change in attainment for each school over their performance six years prior to the new building. While each FCBS school has taken their own route, with natural variations year on year, the downturn seen in the other BSF schools after year two has not materialised.

of these schools came at a time when there was very little knowledge within the industry about what schools need from their buildings. Given the relative immaturity of school construction, it seems important to look into the performance of schools in new buildings, looking for consequential improvements in school educational attainment.

Schools lend themselves to large-scale analysis through their use of standardised tests, in this case GCSEs, which are taken at the end of compulsory education (age 16). These tests are standardised nationally and, with careful controls, can be used to compare schools and progress year-on-year. For this study, we collected data for all English secondary schools from 2000 to 2013, which is openly available from the DfE, and created a sub-set of the BSF schools to look at in greater detail. For this study we specifically used Level 2 performance, representing the percentage of students achieving five or more GCSEs at grade C or above. There are other measures that are widely used, such as progress figures or attainment in English and maths GCSEs, but over this long period only Level 2 attainment was available. Absenteeism data is also widely used in measuring school performance, but due to changing metrics over the past 13 years, longitudinal assessment isn't possible. The only absenteeism metric that can be used over this period is total absenteeism, including authorised absenteeism, which has dropped as schools have become able to fine parents for taking students out of school.

When looking at school performance, it's important to isolate the socio-economic background of the school from the performance, for example in deprived areas attainment is substantially lower than in affluent districts. No two schools operate in identical situations and overlooking this by directly comparing schools would give significantly misleading results.

Similarly, comparison between years needs to be carefully undertaken; we often hear that exams are easier than they used to be. While this is not necessarily true, pass rates do tend to increase year-on-year, so all attainment figures need to be normalised against the national average before looking at trends. While data is available for 2014, due to the significant changes to how non-GCSE exams are included in attainment metrics, the data for this year is not usable.

To understand the performance of schools that received new buildings (or over 80% refurbished), we can start to look at the performance of each school before and after the new building. By looking at the longitudinal path each school has taken, any changes that occur as they move into the new building will be evident. To clearly see any changes, only schools with three years in the new building and six years in the old building have been examined, with the attainment figures normalised against the national average. This created a set of 75 secondary schools that have the full attainment history and received a new building. There were over 550 schools significantly refurbished or entirely rebuilt under the BSF programme, but only 75 had the required data that would enable analysis. We think it's important to point out that these schools represent the first schools built under the BSF programme, with many of the design and procurement processes still in their infancy.

Looking at the cumulative progress of the BSF schools (the purple line in Fig 1), there is a clear dip in performance three years before the new building, before improving prior to the new building. Following a slight dip after the move to the new building, possibly caused by the disruption of moving into the new building, then the results improve further, then sharply dip. Given that the school improves prior to the move to the new building, it is clear that there is some part of the process of getting a new building under the BSF programme that causes the school to improve. This may be a consequence of the increased focus on the school (similar to the Hawthorne effect) or that part of the local authority administration of BSF included improving the school. It's also clear that the schools were already underperforming (shown by the drop in performance three years prior to the new building) so may have had a greater capacity to improve. It is likely that the schools selected to receive new buildings were the schools in desperate need of improvement, with the local authority recognising the BSF programme could act as a catalyst to improve the school.

Perhaps the most interesting, and rather depressing aspect of the school performance is that deterioration in the third year of the new building, with the mean performance dropping to a point close to six years prior to the new building. Looking at this process it would be tempting to say that any improvement in the school performance is due to whatever processes were used prior to the occupation of the new building (that caused the initial improvement). However, not all the schools' performance regressed in year 3, there are still some schools way above average.[1] Looking at FCBS schools in Fig 1, the general trend from the 11 schools analysed is considerably better than the national average. Although the number of schools is much smaller and we do not have the same length of data for the FCBS schools, the performance improvement appears to be sustained beyond the simple move into the new building. A majority of the schools in Fig 2 are academies, which are fundamentally different from the typical schools within the BSF programme, but the process of improvement would be broadly similar.

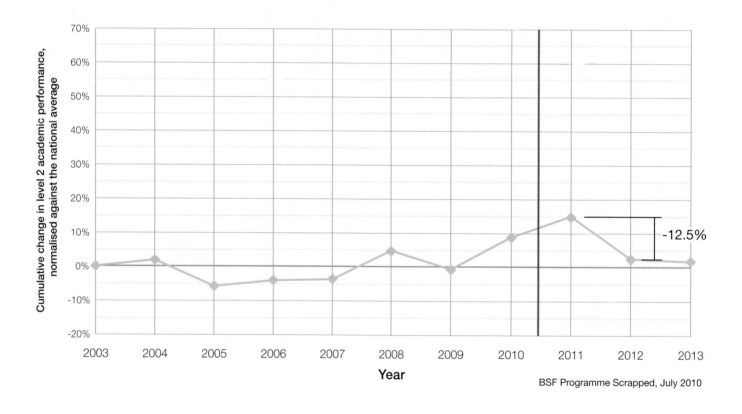

BSF Programme Scrapped, July 2010

Fig 2 The cumulative average percentage of students achieving five or more GCSEs at grade C or more in the schools that had their BSF schools scrapped in July 2010 from a sample of 310 schools out of a total 715 schools.

As with any entity as complex as a school, understanding the exact mechanism that creates any change in performance is difficult and this study only identifies relative changes to school improvement. What we can see from the performance study is that the process of building a new school improves the performance, and that within FCBS schools this appears to be more sustainable. We ourselves are aware of which lines represent which schools, and we know some of the reasons for the sharp rises or falls in attainment, generally due to changes in leadership, and we must also acknowledge that not all schools necessarily improve year on year. The general trends for our schools are satisfying, but it is difficult to learn specifics from such generic information.

To try to understand the difference the new building makes, we extended our analysis to look at the schools that were promised new buildings under BSF, but were let down once the government changed in 2010, with the BSF programme scrapped in July of that year. We see that same improvement in student attainment leading up to a new building, based on the hope that the new building brings, before a sad decline in performance one year after the announcement. The continued improvement in 2011 is difficult to explain, but is likely caused by the hope created through the ongoing legal challenge mounted by six councils over the premature end of the BSF programme, but which ultimately failed to force the government to provide the new buildings they were promised. This is the biggest change in school performance over the ten year period, either positive or negative. For all the political bluster of a new government, when promises are broken by politicians there are very real repercussions. Any short-term gains in popularity or the budget are undermined by the long-term detrimental effect on the education of society.

A recent study of primary schools by Barrett et al measured the various aspects of the built environment (air quality, light levels, colour, etc) and compared the difference in performance between the schools.[2] Their findings show that the built environment accounts for 25% of the academic performance of the students, with the rest coming from the staff at the school. Primary schools are very different from the secondary schools we have been looking at, but they give a good idea of the importance of buildings in student attainment. However, a new school building doesn't just impact the occupants through the environment, it also has the ability to attract new teachers. For a school that is struggling, a new building can be the catalyst to overcome any latent inertia, reinventing themselves with a new image, staff, or teaching vision. This dip following a new building may be a consequence of the school leadership struggling to maintain that impetus, either through changing staff or growing complacency within the school. Within the FCBS schools, those with a noticeable dip tend to be those who have leadership changes after the move to the new building. Making this transformation endure is the challenge that school leaders face, with the building there to support and encourage their vision. With completely new schools, they are in an ideal position to create an inspiring, new approach to teaching, without the need for transformation of practices from pre-existing schools. Life can be easier with a blank canvas.

1. The Hawthorne effect (or observer effect) is the change in behaviour that occurs when being observed, for example people will work harder when they know their output is being measured. The effect is named after the Hawthorne Works, and described in the 1950s by Henry A Landsberger while looking back at studies on the effect of lighting in the work place from the 1920s and 1930s by another researcher Elton Mayo, an industrial researcher.
2. Barrett, P, Y Zhang, J Moffat, K Kobbacy, "An holistic, multi-level analysis identifying the impact of classroom design on pupils' learning", *Build Environ*, 59, 2013, pp 678–689.

CONCLUSIONS

ENERGY USE

JOE JACK WILLIAMS AND IAN TAYLOR

While school buildings are there to enable education, we cannot overlook their wider impact on the environment. Perhaps the most readily measureable impact is the CO_2 emitted as a consequence of the building's energy use. Given the number of schools built under the recent BSF programme, it provides a good opportunity to see how they compare to the existing building stock. Fortunately, through the government's Display Energy Certificate (DEC) programme, the energy consumption of all public buildings over a certain size (initially 1,000 m^2, but now 500 m^2) are required to record and display their energy consumption figures using a standardised methodology. DECs record overall energy use for the building per square metre, with the final reported energy consumption falling into two categories of energy use: electricity and heating (including domestic hot water).

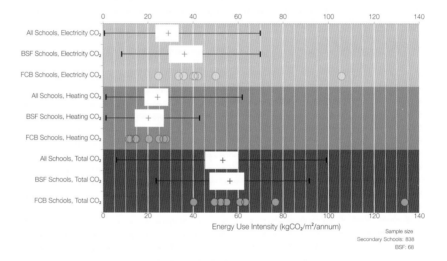

Box and whisker plot comparing the distributions of carbon emissions by existing, BSF and FCBS schools in England, using display energy certificates (DECs) data from 2012.

Using the methodology from Hong and Steadman, we can create a cumulative frequency graph of the energy usage for existing secondary schools during the academic year ending in 2012.[1] Because not all schools have lodged valid DECs for this period, we have a total of 838 schools included in this study out of around 3,200 secondary schools in England. While it is difficult to put an exact figure on the number of projects built under the BSF programme, somewhere between 550 and 600 buildings were replaced or significantly refurbished. The BSF programme formally closed in 2010, but projects continued to be completed for up to three years after this date. From these completed schools, 68 BSF projects lodged a valid DEC in 2012 which have been overlaid on the existing school energy graph. The cumulative frequency graph shows the distribution of energy usage, with the median average usage at the 50%. To help compare the BSF schools with the existing stock, a box plot has been added to the graph showing the distribution of each set of schools. The central box represents the inter-quartile range, showing where 50% of the schools are found, with the cross giving the mean average and the whiskers representing the minimum and maximum.

Looking at the graph we can start to see that the new BSF schools are generally emitting less CO_2 through heating than the rest of the building stock by 4 kg CO_2/m²/annum. This is not surprising as the new buildings were subject to minimum fabric standards that prevent heat loss from the buildings. Coupled with new, efficient heating systems, it is clear why the heating energy use in new buildings is less than in the existing buildings. Focusing on the FCBS schools, those using the most energy are the buildings that have a mix of heating systems and consequently complex controls. For example, one school has difficulty isolating the underfloor heating from the rest of the system, resulting in the whole heating system activating during the underfloor heating system warm-up period, wasting significant amounts of energy. Another of the schools consuming more energy than expected, uses warm air heating, driven by the need to fully mechanically ventilate the whole building. While this reduces the installation complexity, it is performing less efficiently than more typical wet systems. Those FCBS schools using lower amounts of heating energy tend to have more efficient control systems, with the school using the least heating energy having distributed plant rooms to serve each teaching wing.

Conversely, the BSF schools use on average nearly 25% more electricity than the existing buildings. While this is disappointing, given the additional technology in the new schools, increase in electricity use in new school buildings was somewhat inevitable. Many new buildings have received dedicated server rooms to run the intensive ICT equipment throughout the school, from interactive whiteboards, to tablets, to high density computer suites. Difficulty in meeting strict acoustic requirements pushed many buildings towards mechanical ventilation, which inherently uses more electricity than simple openable windows. This high electricity use is compounded by metering issues at many schools that prevents any renewable technologies (solar PV for example) from being deducted from the overall electricity use. The FCBS schools using the most energy tend to have a mix of mechanically and naturally ventilated spaces, but tend to be clustered around the BSF schools. A study into one school identified 40% of the overall electricity use was through small-power and lighting, both highly linked to occupant behaviour. At the very top of the electricity line, one FCBS school exposes a flaw in the DEC methodology, as a majority of the energy is used to electrically heat temporary classrooms, but this has been classified as separate to the heating load. However this does raise an interesting issue about future expansion of schools, an occurrence that may be more prevalent with an increasing population.

The increased electricity usage causes the overall carbon emissions of the new BSF buildings to be marginally higher than the existing building stock, although not at a statistically significant level. All of the improvements in the building fabric are being offset by the increasing electricity use. This shows the true nature of reducing energy use; enabling and engaging the users so that they control their building in an efficient way. Systems that are intelligible by the user/building manager, such as radiators or openable windows, are much easier to manage in an efficient manner. The reduction in complexity also reduces potential areas for problems, making fault finding easier and the initial commissioning more reliable.

1. Hong, S, Steadman, P, "An Analysis of Display Energy Certificates for Public Buildings, 2008 to 2012". December 2013. Available from https://www. bartlett.ucl.ac.uk/energy/news/documents/CIBSE _Analysis_of_Display_Energy_Certificates_for_ Public_Buildings_.pdf, accessed 20 August 2015.

CONCLUSIONS

LEARNING FROM PUPILS AND TEACHERS

DESIGN AND PRACTICE: HOW NEW SCHOOL BUILDINGS INFLUENCE TEACHERS' AND PUPILS' EXPERIENCE OF SCHOOLING

DANIELS, H, TSE, HM, TANZI NETO, A, STABLES, A, ORTEGA, L, AND COX, S (2015).

This chapter is drawn from an ongoing study of ten new secondary schools built over the last ten years, five of which were designed by FCBS. The overall project involves the development of a methodology for systematically analysing the relationship of school space to the experiences of students, teachers and parents. It expands notions of post-occupancy evaluation (POE) research by exploring how the intentions of an educational vision which informed an initial school design, the intentions of the final building, and the intentions of those people who occupy that building interact in a way which influences experiences of the end users. Our work is based on the assumption that these intentions will be influenced by wider social and cultural histories.

Our project seeks to understand how and why the educational vision of new schools built under the BSF programme came to fruition and how the vision translated into the final design. The preliminary findings reveal a significant relationship between the characteristics of the design process and everyday practices of the schools. They also are indicative of the way the outcomes of that relationship affects the perceptions of the students, teachers and the wider community.

METHODOLOGY

Our research is based on a five-step, mixed methods design (Greene 2007), collecting data through interview, observation and documentary analysis, capturing both first-person (subjective) and third-person (objective/intersubjective) perspectives over the phases of the project. The sample of schools consists of 15 examples of different secondary designs including five examples of 'traditional' schools used as control schools in our data analysis.

This preliminary report focuses on the difficult transition from primary to secondary schools and on the pupils concerns prior to and immediately after making this transition. We have studied the degree of connectedness that students feel with their school environment looking at both new schools and control schools. We have also summarised some wider conclusions from our more extensive studies relating to the process of developing a new school and the importance of inclusive consultation.

THE PUPILS' PERSPECTIVE

We spoke to Year 6 pupils in their final weeks of primary schooling. In our wider project all students who were moving to the new schools (240 students) were asked about what they thought would be different about their new school. In a dataset of 1,828 statements, concerns about the scale of the building predominated, followed by references to social relationships with new friends and new teachers. The data were used to generate the word cloud shown in Fig 1.

There was also evidence of persistent worries about teachers' strictness, bullying, punishments and how to deal with new rules. Less frequently there were concerns with homework, the length of the lessons, harder work, the possibilities of better classes and more sports activities. Concerns with social relations also predominate in the accounts given by pupils on the verge of secondary transfer. The size and scale of the building is a significant concern. We followed these pupils into their secondary schools and their teachers asked them to write an essay about "My first week in school". Again issues concerning social relations predominated along with accounts of navigating their new school environments as shown below.

EXAMPLES OF REFERENCES TO SOCIAL RELATIONS

> I got to make loads of friends... hopefully I or anyone else won't get bullied....
> Finding my way was the hardest bit of it....
> I thought the older kids would pick on me....
> I felt like everyone was acting older than what they are....
> My friend was in the same class as me so at least I knew someone....

EXAMPLES OF REFERENCES TO NAVIGATING THE NEW ENVIRONMENT

> I didn't know where to go....
> It's just trying to remember where all the rooms are....
> I told the teacher I was lost he said it was ok....
> Big adventure going through every corridor and finding my way out again....
> I did get lost a few times....

During these early days in Year 7 of their new school, pupils were asked to make a list of places that were important to them. Word Cloud 2 in Fig 2 depicts these data.

The rank order of places was as follows: sports hall, library, art, MUGA (multi-use games area), music, drama, outside, toilets. References to the library were the subject of a considerable amount of follow up discussion eg.

> There aren't many quiet places in the school: I think we picked it [library] cause its quiet place where you can sit down and read. So what you can do is bury your troubles in a book.

> Loads of people go to the library at lunch time and there's this room there where you can be on your own, it's just the best.

We argue that these data along with other findings suggest that the importance of spaces for social relations, social learning and respite are very important in secondary school design. The library is of particular importance as are sports areas. Students stated that they valued the library space because it afforded both a quiet place to work in the company of friends as well as a quiet place to 'get away from' the hurly-burly of school life.

In schools where they did not feel that their behaviour was the explicit object of adult observation then students spoke of their liking for so-called 'heart spaces' in which they could enjoy the company of their peers in safety. There is an important difference to mark here. If they felt that their behaviour was being scrutinised and over-controlled then we noted that they did not use such spaces. However students in schools which were felt to be trusting of them used these spaces and felt pleased to be in a situation where they could be observed as this ensured that they were in a safe environment.

SCHOOL CONNECTEDNESS

School connectedness has been defined by Goodenow (1993), as "the extent to which students feel personally accepted, respected, included and supported by others in the school social environment" (p 80). This construct is argued to be particularly important for adolescents as they rely less on the family as part of the individuation process and come to rely more on extrafamilial relationships such as those found in schools, with friends and others (Goodenow, 1993).

A "School Connectedness" questionnaire was used to gather data from all pupils at the end of Year 6 (in the primary school), during the first two weeks of Year 7 in the secondary school and at the end of Year 7. The questionnaire is based on a short form of the Psychological Sense of School Membership Scale (Goodenow, 1993) which assesses the extent to which students feel accepted, valued, respected and included in school. The scale used consisted of 11 items each rated on a five-point scale to indicate how strongly they endorse each item.

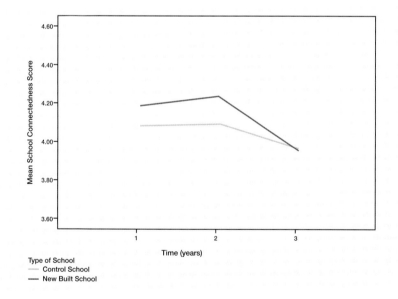

Fig 3 Trajectories of School Connectedness over Time. Time 1: Primary School Year 6 Term 3; Time 2: Secondary School Year 7 Term 1; Time 3: Secondary School Year 7 Term 3.

Fig 3 shows the results aggregated across all schools. Whilst the large standard errors in the data preclude assertions about overall effects, there are significant differences in favour of new built schools with regard to feelings of safety during break/lunchtime at the beginning of the year of Year 7 and also that it was easy for them to find their way around the school at the end of Year 7 as we will show below.

Pupils in 'all-through' schools where there is primary and secondary provision on the same site found it easier to find their way around the school at the beginning of Year 7, than their peers who had come from separate primary schools.

When compared with the primary school (Time 1 Year 6) data for new-build secondary-only schools show a significant positive effect in for scores against the statement that they "can have time on their own in the school if they wanted to" at the beginning of the Year 7, and that they felt proud of belonging to that specific school by the end of Year 7 and they also felt safe in their school during lessons although this effect dissapated by the end of Year 7.

The data show that student connectedness to the new building was high on the category of personal wellbeing. Pupils said that they felt safe during break/lunchtime, during lessons and that they could have time on their own in the school if they wanted to.

These findings echo the findings from the essay data and the lists of important places in that they affirm the importance of social space which can be used in safety. Importantly, designs with high levels of internal visibility can afford such spaces but only when the practices of the school are conducive to the formation of feelings of trust and safety. Safety, trust and belonging are intertwined within the complex relations of design and practice.

CONCLUSIONS

Our data suggest that the relation between design and practice is crucial to the production of a building which can be and is used effectively. There are three elements to this relationship. Firstly, it is more likely that a successful occupation and use of a building results when the practices that the occupying staff wish to follow mirror the principles of practice that are embedded in the vision and design. Secondly, this is most evident when the eventual practitioners (usually the headteacher who takes over the school building on completion) have been involved in an inclusive consultation process throughout the vision, design and construction process. Thirdly, it is quite clear that the principles of the brief may be regarded differently by different individual and professional groups. This may seek to compound problems with the relationship between design and practice.

> The design is a provocation to learn differently but it's what you do inside it that matters.
> **HEADTEACHER FROM ONE SAMPLE SCHOOL.**

The second point relates to the processes of transition between primary and secondary school. Rice et al (2011) review the evidence on the educational and emotional challenges that young people face in the transition from primary to secondary school. The findings of their research suggest that transition policies "should recognise the importance of both the formal and informal social systems involved" (p 47). Our school connectedness data suggest that when they first arrive in secondary school young people find it is easy to find their way around a new-build school, they feel safer at break and lunchtimes and also find it easier to have time on their own if they want to. By the end of their first year in their newly built secondary schools they feel more proud of belonging to their school and safer in these schools during lesson time than their peers in old-build schools. They rated 'all-through' schools easier to navigate than secondary only schools. The overall, although not statistically significant, trend is for the new-build data to show a higher global connectedness score on entry although this benefit appears to dissipate over the course of a school year.

A recent study by West et al (2010, p 21) noted that the primary—secondary transition is widely understood as 'one of the most difficult in pupils' educational careers' (Zeedyk et al, 2003, 67) and, more broadly, as a 'key rite of passage' (Pratt and George, 2005, 16) in young people's lives. Given this consensus on the difficulty that this transition poses then our research suggests a broader consideration of the importance of the design and the structure ('all-through' versus separate) of schools is worthy of attention.

Finally, our attention has been drawn to the ways in which control is exercised in the practice of schooling. All the new-build schools we have worked with have high levels of visibility incorporated as a design feature. In some practices we have observed ways in which this is subverted through the judicious application of posters on glass walls and windows. In some schools there was a very explicit focus on desirable behaviour. This arose in settings in which there was not an inclusive consultation process. The BSF design principles were predicated on an assumption of enhanced levels of autonomy. These were not aligned with the practices of the schools and young people tended not to use observable spaces during times of informal social activity. Whereas in an approach in which the major pedagogic preoccupation was with attainment the young people happily populated open, visible space at social times within the school day. Even if their teachers did not particularly like the design of the school their focus remained primarily on educational outcomes. Our analysis of these matters is incomplete but we feel that the data suggest a complex relation between practices of design and construction, relations of control within the practices of occupation and the use of space. Visibility within a building may be seen as beneficial in enacting a regime of high control or, alternatively, as a means of forming and fostering community.

These conclusions lead us to form a general argument that one design may be perceived and used in very different ways in different practices of schooling. We also argue that good design requires good multi-professional holistic post-occupancy evaluation which has a remit that goes far beyond the physical functioning of the building. An understanding of social relations that are enacted within a design as it is taken up by different forms of practice is crucial to the development of better sites for schooling.

There are several emerging themes within our as yet incomplete research:

A.Strong integration of the teachers pedagogy into the design of the school gives rise to a better occupation, and orientation on the part of the staff to learn how to use the building.

B. When staff come into a building that they've had no part in designing, and they don't necessarily have an affiliation to the intended practice they remain retrospective in their view and do everything they can to recreate a building that lends itself to traditional teaching.

C.Ideas of personalisation in traditional schools can lead to a desire for bigger (single) classrooms with breakout space NOT large open areas. But they also said that their traditional building is currently inhibiting what they want to do.

D.When there is a disconnect between the orientation of the occupying pedagogy and the design of the building then a child will feel less connected to the school.

LESSONS FROM PUPILS AND TEACHERS

- Social spaces and social learning in schools are important for students and may be undervalued in design and practice.
- Inclusive consultation is a vital component of the processes of design, construction and occupation.
- Design, and features of design, may assume very different forms of significance and have very different effects in different practices of occupation.
- On leaving primary school, students have major concerns about the social relations, scale and navigation of the secondary schools they are about to enter.
- Colour, clear organisation diagrams and the provision of spaces for learning and being can ease this transition.
- This easing of concerns will only be achieved if the practices envisioned or anticipated by the design are witnessed in the practices of occupation.
- Buildings alone do not transform practice. Transformation arises in the interplay between the two. For example, designs with high internal visibility may be used to create a sense of community or be experienced as forms of intrusive surveillance.
- This understanding calls for a greater degree of engagement between designers and practitioners in the construction of school.

References

- DfES, *Building Schools for the Future: A new approach to capital investment*, London, DfES, 2004.
- DfES, *Building Schools for the Future: Consultation on a new approach to capital investment*, London, DfES, 2003.
- Goodenow, C, "The psychological sense of school membership among adolescents: Scale development and educational correlates", *Psychology in the Schools*, 30, 1993, pp 79–90.
- Greene, JC,"Is Mixed Methods Social Inquiry a Distinctive Methodology?", *Journal of Mixed Methods Research*, 2, 1, 2008, pp 7–22.
- James, S, *Review of education capital*, London, DfE, 2011.
- National Audit Office, "The Building Schools for the Future Programme: Renewing the secondary school estate", Report HC 135 Session, 2008–2009.

- Pratt S, and R George. "Transferring friendships: Girls' and boys' friendships in the transition from primary to secondary school", *Children and Society* 19, 2005, pp 16–26.
- Rice, F, Frederickson, N, & Seymour, J, "Assessing pupil concerns about transition to secondary school", *British Journal of Educational Psychology*, 81 (2), pp 244–263.
- West, P, Sweeting, H, & Young, R, "Transition matters: pupils' experiences of the primary–secondary school transition in the West of Scotland and consequences being and attainment", *Research papers in education*, 25(1), 2008, pp 21–50.
- Zeedyk, S, J Gallacher, M Henderson, G Hope, B Husband, and K Lindsay, "Negotiating the transition from primary to secondary school: Perceptions of pupils, parents and teachers", *School Psychology International* 24, no. 1: 2003, pp 67–79.

CONCLUSIONS

LESSONS LEARNED

PETER CLEGG

The third generation of state school building has only just begun. In the last ten years we have been rebuilding schools that have suffered from decades of poor maintenance and under-investment but the next ten years are going to see a dramatic rise in the secondary school population the like of which we have not seen since the 1970s. Already there is a shortage of places throughout London at primary school level: before 2020 another 500 secondary schools will be needed to cope with an increase in school-age population (Fig 1). What we have learned from an extraordinary period of experimentation should now be put to good use.

We have tried to summarise some of the lessons (pp 166–167) under four different headings: issues of process, planning, architecture and environmental design. Some of them may seem terse and obvious, but design is so complicated a process that sometimes the obvious can remain elusive.

The process has often been long drawn-out and painful. The BSF process was predicated on questioning not only the future of school buildings but on the impact they could have on the educational process. So discussions brought in educationalists heads, teachers and children in a genuine bid to transform schools by rebuilding them. And what we learned from the process was that any strong pedagogical ideas that influenced the building design would only work if the staff and particularly the headteacher, bought into the ideas and had the capacity to inspire change. We have seen schools where a radical, open-plan architectural approach failed because it was not embraced by pre-existing school staff. But we have also seen successful new schools, such as the Plymouth School of Creative Arts where new staff, adopt a radical pedagogy which has a symbiotic relationship with a new building, and where the educational philosophy impacted upon the building which in turn impacts positively on the education.

opposite Plymouth School of Creative Arts, © Hufton+Crow.

Fig 1 Graph of school-age population from 1950 to 2030, based on data from the Office of National Statistics. A dramatic increase is expected between 2015 and 2020, similiar to increases experienced in the late 1950s and 1970s.

Ten principles of good school design

1/ Good clear organisation, an easily legible plan, and full accessibility.

2/ Spaces that are well proportioned, efficient, fit for purpose and meet the needs of the curriculum.

3/ Circulation that is well organised, and sufficiently generous.

4/ Good environmental conditions throughout, including appropriate levels of natural light and ventilation.

5/ Attractiveness in design, comparable to that found in other quality public buildings, to inspire pupils, staff and parents.

6/ Good use of the site, and public presence as a civic building wherever possible to engender local pride.

7/ Attractive external spaces with a good relationship to internal spaces and offering appropriate security and a variety of different settings.

8/ A layout that encourages broad community access and use out of hours, where appropriate.

9/ Robust materials that are attractive, that will weather and wear well and that are environmentally friendly.

10/ Flexible design that will facilitate changes in policy and technology and which allows expansion or contraction in the future, where appropriate.

Fig 2 *Achieving well designed schools through PFI: A client guide*, London: CABE (the Commission for Architecture and the Built Environment) 2004. Foreword by Richard Feilden.

The planning of a new school is very dependent on its location and site. Planning new buildings around existing institutions often entails a complex and disruptive phasing strategy and condemns a school to being a building site for several years. Often, since the best location on the site is occupied by the original school, it can result in a complex phasing process. It is only when the new buildings are finally revealed by the demolition of the old that the complex jigsaw is complete. The need for new school places often occurs in urban areas, however, where sites are very rarely available and very expensive. Some of the most successful schools we have built have sprung from these constraints. The Chelsea Academy site is so small there is virtually no part of the site that is not built upon and the roofspaces become the playspaces. Elsewhere, at Aston and Plymouth we are beginning to see the school as new urban typology: multi-level and deep-plan, with complex light wells and an embracing street presence.

The recommended space budget that we have been dealing with over the last ten years has risen and fallen with the ambitions and preoccupations of the government-sponsored targets. Pre-BSF it was the paucity of these standards as well as the poor design aspirations that led to the outrage against the quality of new schools delivered during the 1990s, and to the CABE sponsored initiative (led by Richard Feilden) to define the qualities of a good school. The "ten principles of good school design" are as relevant today as they were ten years ago (Fig 2). But during the intervening years it became apparent, to many architects, and eventually the Department of Education, that space standards were not high enough to deliver the flexibility and quality that was demanded resulting in an increase of about 10% in overall areas per pupil. With the ending of the BSF process by a Tory government, the space standards were again reduced, heralding a return to the lowest common denominator of school design: the narrow, double-loaded corridor of classrooms. For teachers space is one of the most precious aspects of school design, and it is difficult to extend classrooms. Small spaces, low ceilings and narrow corridors are the attributes that led us to decide on the demolition of 1960s buildings: it will be tragic if our generation are seen to be making the same mistakes, and now, as the latest generation of schools are already talking about expansion we realise that one of the issues we have not addressed adequately is expandability.

Some of the major changes that have been ushered in by BSF (and subsequently ushered out by its cancellation) are in the field of environmental design. We understand better the relationship between daylight, glare and solar gain, though we still have problems with the latter. We have improved ventilation standards and devised ways of achieving them. And we have invested hugely in an improved acoustical environment. We have also learned more about energy consumption in our schools, with significant reductions in heating bills, but this has been countered by a significant increase in energy consumption, predominantly IT based, which has meant that our ambition for zero carbon schools has been thwarted. As architects we have done almost all we can with building fabric to reduce carbon emissions. There remains the challenge of reducing embodied energy and working with schools to reduce the performance gap between the anticipated and actual carbon emissions.

Of all the lessons, however, the most humbling for architects is that aspiration and inspiration, derived from leadership and teachers themselves have a much greater impact on performance outcomes than the physical school environment. We can facilitate good education and create flexible spaces to suit different teaching approaches. We can provide a healthy, enlightening school environment, and create buildings that inspire and delight. But our research shows that the contribution a new building makes to academic performance is overshadowed by the influence of teachers and particularly headteachers, and the promise of a new school seems to generate a greater improvement in attainment than tends to happen after its delivery. It appears that simply focussing attention and offering help can begin to alleviate a problem, whether one is dealing with underperforming children or schools.

This shouldn't come as a surprise to me. My father, who was an educationalist, and commissioned new schools in the last school building boom of the 1960s, always used to praise the teachers whose extraordinary talents managed to overcome the adversity of desperately poor school buildings often in areas of social deprivation. He was an advocate of mindfulness in the educational process and it is probably appropriate therefore to finish with a story he used to tell about how to get the best out of any young person, in this case the sculptor Michelangelo (who was not a bad architect either!). When the young Michaelangelo first came to Rome, he brought with him some gifts and a note from one of his tutors which said:

> The bearer of these presents the sculptor Michelangelo. His nature is such that he needs to be drawn out by kindness and encouragement, but if love be shown him and he be treated really well he will accomplish things that will make the whole world wonder.

Ultimately it is the gift of attentiveness and love that is at the heart of the educational process. It takes great buildings and great teachers to make a great school.

1/
PROCESS

- We are designing schools for 50 or so years during which time pedagogical ideas will come and go. A good school is designed to meet the needs of its first generation of teachers and children but not prejudice the opportunities for future generations to teach in a different way.

- Some headteachers are too busy or not interested in the idea of a new school: others have real vision. But someone needs to champion the educational agenda for any new building; preferably someone with a tolerance for a variety of new approaches to pedagogy.

- With tight budgets in an era of austerity, spend the money on space and allow the potential for future upgrades on equipment and finishes. Don't cut classroom areas as this reduces the flexibility of the individual teacher.

- Openness and security are key issues in school design. It is very easy for the trust in children to break down and a more disciplinarian system to be imposed by excessive staff presence. Maximising passive supervision and transparency can really help.

- Data shows that the promise of a new school can lift performance, more than the school itself and that the influence of the headteacher can have more of an impact on attainment and attendance than a new school building. Often the new environment has a positive impact for a few years but improvement can be short-lived.

- Where there is a legacy of working with an existing school it is more difficult to effect transformation in teaching methods. New schools with new heads and a radical approach to education can more easily create changes in pedagogy.

- Phasing the building of new schools on pre-existing sites can be time consuming, disruptive and costly. It is often inevitable but needs to be built into all proposals from the outset.

- Consult widely and meaningfully: new schools need to be embedded into their community, but design for the long-term future, not to meet short-term preoccupations.

2/
PLANNING

- Every school needs a sense of place: a focal space which embodies its sense of community and identity. It can be the assembly hall, a main entrance, a play area or a dining area, but it helps with the idea of collective ownership and provides a heart for the institution.

- The sheer size of a secondary school can be intimidating to the youngest children in transition from primary school. Breaking down the institutionality of the school by creating a smaller dedicated Year 7 area or a series of 'schools within schools' can reduce this sense of alienation.

- Classrooms around a shared base can work and give flexibility in teaching but the staff have to know how to use the spaces and buy into the concept of team teaching to really make them work.

- While most children appear happy in a relatively boisterous environment, opportunities for quietness and reflectivity need to be provided.

- Toilets are also areas which seem to encourage antisocial behaviour. This can be dramatically reduced by using single cubicles accessible from discrete but supervised circulation spaces, rather than separate blocks of boys and girls toilets.

- In tight urban sites it is possible to maximise the use of space by using sports hall roofs as multi-use games areas (the areas required are virtually identical).

- Most schools have a desire for bigger assembly spaces than a standard EFA space budget will allow for. Combining the drama studio space as a stage to an assembly hall, with acoustic partitioning between the two, can add to the capacity and flexibility of the 'school hall'.

- We often make the mistake of thinking a new school is optimal in size and unlikely to grow. In reality, change is the only constant, and it is important to allow and envisage areas of expansion for new buildings. The demand can come very quickly.

3/
ARCHITECTURE

- Beware anyone who wants an instant 'wow factor': icons are short-lived. Schools need to be robust, flexible and timeless.

- A reasonable amount of transparency really works between shared areas and classrooms, allowing for passive supervision views and daylight, and adding to the sense of the school as one organism.

- Tight corridors and staircases, particularly unsupervised ones, can be a source of bullying. Corridors, if they are needed, should be wide and gracious, staircases open and generous. Passive supervision helps reduce behavioural problems.

- Daylight and view can enhance the quality of otherwise introverted school spaces: a view to the sky, or at the end of a corridor can provide a welcome connection to the outside world.

- Weather protected outdoor spaces help with managing lunchtimes and breaktimes, providing fresh air and a change of environment for children and staff.

- Long-term flexibility is provided by a simple concrete column structure with columns at about nine metre centres, no downstand beams and two-way spanning flat slabs which allow partitions to be located anywhere. Additional height adds to future flexibility.

- Getting children in and out of school is a potential source of behavioural difficulties and irate visiting parents can also cause problems. It can help to open up a number of entrances at the beginning and end of the day with one, carefully controlled front entrance to provide a 'front door' to the school.

- Our research shows that children are extraordinarily perceptive about the qualities of the space they occupy, the colours, finishes and materials that make up their environment. Don't underestimate their interest in the architecture and design of their schools.

4/
ENVIRONMENT

- All mechanical and electrical systems need to be foolproof and allow for human interaction that is not necessarily consistent or sensible. Keep it simple!

- Most new schools perform better than average in terms of heating energy consumption and worse than average in terms of electrical energy consumption. The biggest increase is in catering and IT loads, but lighting is still a major culprit.

- Avoid solar overheating by keeping the percentage areas of glazing down to about 30% on southerly elevations and 40% on northerly elevations, and using low solar transmission factor glazing. Most classrooms use whiteboards or projection of some kind and require a low level of light along the teaching wall.

- Of all the (so-called) renewable energy systems, ground-source heat pumps have been the most successful and reliable. Beware biomass heating: it brings problems of supply, cost and maintenance.

- Don't cut the acoustical absorption out of the budget, particularly in hard surfaced and noisy areas such as dining halls. It is vital to the success of any form of open-plan teaching.

- Allow the building to breathe. In naturally ventilated buildings it is relatively easy to achieve acoustically attenuated airpaths from classroom to corridor to help enhance cross-ventilation.

- Thermally heavyweight buildings are less likely to overheat: exposed concrete on the ceiling can act as a thermal damper, and also provide some summertime cooling.

- The route to low carbon design: halve the demand, double the equipment efficiency, decarbonise the fuel supply and monitor performance. Zero carbon needs to become a shared mission between designers, contractors and users.

PROJECT CREDITS

NORTHAMPTON ACADEMY

Alina White
Amos Goldreich
Carol James
David Saxby
Eve Goldman
Ian Taylor
Jennie Green-Walker
Joerg Majer
Jonathon Mitchell
Ray Kearney
Richard Feilden
Ron Nkomba
Trevor Brown
Anne Bodkin—Post-Occupancy Evaluation
Joe Jack Williams—Post-Occupancy Evaluation

SPONSORS/ United Learning Trust and DCSF

CONTRACTOR/ Miller Construction

STRUCTURAL ENGINEER/ Buro Happold

M&E ENGINEER/ Buro Happold

COST CONSULTANT/ CM Parker Browne

LANDSCAPE CONSULTANTS/ Plincke Landscape

ST MARY MAGDALENE ACADEMY

Aelene Thorne
Alina White
Amos Goldreich
Andrew Macintosh
Claire Smith
George Wilson
Helen Roberts
Ian Taylor
Jason Cornish
Julia Wedel
Larissa Johnston
Lynton Pepper
Marigold Webster
Rachel Calladine
Ray Kearney
Richard Battye
Ron Nkomba

SPONSORS/ London Diocesan Board for Schools in conjunction with DCSF

PROJECT MANAGER/ EC Harris

CONTRACTOR/ Mace Plus

STRUCTURAL ENGINEER/ Buro Happold

M&E ENGINEER/ Buro Happold

COST CONSULTANT/ Davis Langdon

LANDSCAPE CONSULTANTS/ Churchman Landscape Architects

CHELSEA ACADEMY

John Southall
Marigold Webster
Paul Priest
Peter Clegg
Rachel Sayers
Ron Nkomba
Tim den Dekker
Tobias Stiller
Will Jefferies

SPONSORS/ RBKC (Royal Borough of Kensington and Chelsea) and LDBS (London Diocesan Board for Schools)

CONTRACTOR/ Wates Construction

ORIGINATING DESIGN STRUCTURAL ENGINEER/ Price & Myers

ORIGINATING DESIGN M&E ENGINEER/ Fulcrum Consulting

COST CONSULTANT/ Davis Langdon LLP

LANDSCAPE CONSULTANTS/ Churchman Landscape Architects

ASTON UNIVERSITY ENGINEERING ACADEMY

Alison Hesketh
Anahita Chouhan
Christine Skaar
David Stansfield
Martin Hedges
Michael Woodford
Olivia Hough
Steve Wilby

SPONSOR/ Aston University

CONTRACTOR/ Lend Lease

STRUCTURAL AND CIVIL ENGINEER/ Cox Turner Morse Limited

M&E AND ACOUSTIC ENGINEER/ Cundall

COST CONSULTANT/ Lend lease

LANDSCAPE ARCHITECT/ Planit

HIGHFIELD HUMANITIES COLLEGE

Alex Whitbread
Alison Ho
George Wilson
Keith Bradley
Marigold Webster
Richard Priest
Simon Richardson

DRAPERS' ACADEMY

Andrew Macintosh
Chris Allen
Clarissa Yee
Ian Taylor
Jeremy Yu
John Southall
Nyla Hussain
Rachel Sayers
Richard Battyc
Rory Martin

CLIENT/ Blackpool Local Education Partnership (a public private partnership between Blackpool Council, The Eric Wright Group and Northgate Management Services)

CONTRACTOR/ Eric Wright Construction

STRUCTURAL ENGINEER/ Booth King Partnership Ltd

M&E ENGINEER/ RPS Group

COST CONSULTANT/ Eric Wright Construction

LANDSCAPE ARCHITECT/ Plincke Landscape

SPONSORS/ The Drapers' Company and Queen Mary University

PROJECT MANAGER/ EC Harris

CONTRACTOR/ Kier Construction London

STRUCTURAL ENGINEER/ WSP UK

M&E ENGINEER/ WSP UK

COST CONSULTANT/ Kier Construction London

LANDSCAPE CONSULTANT/ EDCO Design London

WILLIAM PERKIN CHURCH OF ENGLAND HIGH SCHOOL

Agata Baranowska

Helen Roberts

Ian Taylor

Jacob Szikora

Jo Gimenez

John Southall

Luke Gilbert

Marigold Webster

Michael Baumgartner

Ray Kearney

Ron Nkomba

Rory Martin

CLIENT/ Twyford Church of England Academies Trust, sponsored by London Diocesan Board for Schools

CONTRACTOR/ Kier

STRUCTURAL ENGINEER/ AECOM

CLT SUBCONTRACTOR/ KLHUK (and Ramboll as Structural Consultants to KLHUK)

M&E ENGINEERING/ KPE

COST CONSULTANT/ Kier also managed costs and budgets

LANDSCAPE ARCHITECT/ EDCO Design Limited

PLYMOUTH SCHOOL OF CREATIVE ARTS

Alan Keane

Andy Theobald

Colin Cobb

Matt Barrass

Tom Jarman

SPONSORS/ Plymouth College of Arts

CONTRACTOR/ Kier Construction

STRUCTURAL ENGINEER/ Jubb Consulting

M&E ENGINEER/ Aecom

COST CONSULTANT/ Gleeds

LANDSCAPE CONSULTANTS/ Rathbone Partnership

BIOGRAPHIES

FEILDEN CLEGG BRADLEY STUDIOS

Feilden Clegg Bradley Studios is an architecture practice founded in 1978 by Peter Clegg and Richard Feilden.

From its base in Bath it has expanded to have studios in three other cities: London, Manchester and Belfast. The practice has always been involved with educational projects, working for schools in the public and private sectors, as well as a variety of higher education projects both at home and abroad. Secondary schools in the state sector began with the award-winning John Cabot CTC, completed more than 20 years ago, and in the last 15 years the practice has completed more than 20 schools which form the basis of 'lessons learned' in this book. FCBStudios has won 14 RIBA awards for schools projects, more than any other practice in the country.

The practice has also learned to live with differing funding regimes, from Academies, to Building Schools for the Future, to the Priority Schools Building Programme. Unfortunately we have seen during the last ten years of austerity a gradual reduction in building cost rates which has meant less attention to the quality of space, materials and details. Along with this has come a reduced ambition from teachers and school providers, so that the radical and transformational potential of new school architecture has been curtailed.

Over the years FCBStudios has developed an approach to education which involves a clear understanding of the aspirations of the current school leadership, but also an appreciation of the constant need for change and rethinking the way education is developed and delivered. So each school is unique to the constraints of its site and context but also to those who are defining its organisation and pedagogy. And the pluralist approach of our work also comes from the many different architects who have enjoyed working on such fulfilling projects.

PETER CLEGG

Peter Clegg is a Founding Partner with Feilden Clegg Bradley Studios, having established the practice with Richard Feilden in 1978. Widely regarded as a pioneer in the field of environmental design, he is actively involved in research, design and education.

Peter was the primary author of *Feilden Clegg Bradley: The Environmental Handbook* (2007), a substantial account of the practice's sustainable design experience over the last 30 years. He also edited the practice's publication *Education: Architecture: Urbanism* (2011), an account of three new university buildings. He is currently a Professor at the University of Bath and Chair of the South West Design Review Panel. He was made a Royal Designer for Industry (RDI) in 2010.

He was Senior Partner in charge of the architectural developments at the Yorkshire Sculpture Park, the Central Office for the National Trust in Swindon, and the refurbishment of the Southbank Centre in London.

Recent work abroad includes a new gallery for the Leventis Foundation in Cyprus, a School of Engineering in Toronto, and a new school residential secondary school in Bangladesh.

Peter comes from a family of educationalists and escaped to become an architect. He has led the work of the practice in the schools sector and has been involved in many of the projects referred to in this book and much of the post-occupancy evaluation of schools buildings.

DEAN HAWKES

Dean Hawkes is emeritus professor of architectural design at the Welsh School of Architecture, Cardiff University and an emeritus fellow of Darwin College, University of Cambridge. He taught and researched at Cambridge from 1965 to 1995. He was Director of the Martin Centre for Architectural and Urban Studies at Cambridge from 1979 to 1987. In 1995 he was appointed Professor of Architectural Design at Cardiff. Following his retirement in 2002 he returned to Cambridge as a fellow of Darwin College. He has held visiting professorships at schools of architecture in Hong Kong, Singapore, Glasgow, Huddersfield and Leicester. His research is in the field of environmental design in architecture. In the 1970s and 80s he undertook pioneering research on the design of environmentally responsive school buildings, in association with the County Architects of both Essex and Hampshire County Councils. His books include, *The Environmental Tradition* (1996), *The Environmental Imagination* (2008), *and Architecture and Climate* (2012). His buildings, in partnership with Stephen Greenberg, have won four RIBA Architecture Awards. In 2002 he was awarded a Leverhulme Emeritus Research Fellowship to study *The Environmental Function of Architecture* and in 2010 he received the RIBA Annie Spink Award in recognition of his contribution to architectural education.

JOE JACK WILLIAMS

Joe Jack William joined us as an engineering doctoral (EngD) researcher in 2010, previously working as an M&E services consultant for Parsons Brinckerhoff Ltd and URS. During his time working as an M&E consultant, Joe worked as designer on a diverse range of projects, including hotels, tall residential buildings and offices. In addition to design, Joe spent considerable time undertaking site surveys, including determining the cooling load for the Palace of Westminster and condition surveys of MOD's international sites.

Wanting to understand buildings further, Joe started his EngD as a collaboration with UCL and Feilden Clegg Bradley Studios in 2010. He focused on understanding the impact of the school environment on the students, initially looking from an energy usage point of view, but moving towards a holistic understanding of the building from the perspective of the students. To undertake this, he developed a national level database of all the secondary schools in England and a new occupant feedback tool. These allow the impact of the school environment to be analysed at both a high and low level. As part of his role at FCBS, Joe uses the occupant feedback tool within the post-occupancy evaluation framework he has developed.

HARRY DANIELS

Harry Daniels currently holds The Professorship of Education at the Oxford University Department of Education having held Chairs at the Universities of Bath and Birmingham.
He also holds positions as:

- Adjunct Professor, Griffith Institute for Education Research, Griffith University, Brisbane, Australia.
- Research Professor, Centre for Human Activity Theory, Kansai University, Osaka, Japan.
- Research Professor in Cultural Historical Psychology, Moscow State University of Psychology and Education.

His thinking is influenced by theories of the social formation of mind and cultural transmission. This has been developed over the last 25 years through a series of studies on processes and practices of collaboration and marginalisation. He is particularly interested in the mutual shaping of social and cultural organisations and human activity. His projects have included considerations of how patients learn about their disease following a diagnosis of cancer; how professionals learn to do multiagency working and the effects of group administered Cognitive Behavioural Therapy on anxiety and depression in junior school children.

He is editor of *Emotional and Behavioural Difficulty* and co-editor of *Learning, Culture and Social Interaction*.

His current major research project is entitled "Design matters? The effects of new schools on students', teachers' and parents' actions and perceptions". He is also working on projects concerned with exclusion from school.

HAU MING TSE

Hau Ming Tse is a Research Fellow in the Department of Education, University of Oxford. She is also Associate Lecturer in the School of Architecture at Oxford Brookes University.

A qualified architect, Hau Ming was educated at the University of Bath; the University of Cambridge and the Architectural Association, London. After graduating, she worked for nine years at David Chipperfield Architects, where she was an Associate Director. Selected projects include the Hepworth Gallery, Wakefield; the headquarters of BBC Scotland, Glasgow and the San Michele Cemetery, Venice.

Contemporary architecture's radical approach and multidisciplinary agenda continue to influence Hau Ming's work. Her research interests explore the relationship between space, perception and the environment, and her work focuses on productive points of interaction and innovation between theory and practice in learning environments. Current field research examines the complex relationship between design and practice in some of the most challenging primary and secondary schools in the UK.

Current Research is based around the research project: "Design Matters?' The effects of new schools on students', teachers' and parents' actions and perceptions". This research project between educationalists and architects focuses on post-occupancy evaluation analysis to evaluate the relationship between school design and students' and teachers' perceptions and use of educational spaces in newly completed secondary schools in the UK.

ACKNOWLEDGEMENTS

Our involvement with schools in the state secondary sector began with the late Richard Feilden who died ten years ago. It was Richard who began the crusade against the lamentably low standard of new school provision that came with the first wave of privately-financed PFI schools about 15 years ago. Richard was then working for the Commission for Architecture and the Built Environment (CABE) and was responsible for many of their publications giving guidance on school design. He was involved in many of the early schools projects that are referenced in this book, though sadly he did not live to see many of them completed. So our primary acknowledgment should go to Richard.

Over the last 20 years we have designed more than 25 new secondary schools, and the knowledge of what works and what does not, particularly within the constraints of limited space and cost budgets is now embedded across a huge number of people within the practice whose work is represented here. Many of us unfortunately lose touch with the schools once they are complete and we are grateful to those who have focused on the post-occupancy studies whose work has helped us reflect on what we have learned.

Producing a book is a bit like an architectural project but with the design and production effort concentrated into a much shorter time. And the design and delivery team for this includes not only the named authors, to whom we are extremely grateful, but also our internal "design and delivery" team led by Fliss Childs, and including Carlos Parrilla, Nick Crane and Harry Hewlett who helped rationalise all the drawings. But the person whose patience has really been tested is Stephanie Sandall who has managed to juggle all the elements of text, drawings and illustrations, coping with seemingly endless revisions from dozens of contributors. Steph has also acted as the conduit to our team of Rachel Pfleger and Duncan McCorquodale at Artifice to whom, yet again, we extend our gratitude.

Finally we are of course indebted to the client, consultant and contractor teams who have worked with us on so many projects, and most of all to the teachers and children who have brought our buildings to life. We hope that we will learn from this generation of school buildings as we did from the first two phases of school buildings during the last century, and from the radical and transformative thought processes that have helped change the nature of our schools over the last ten years.

Artifice books on architecture
10a Acton Street
London WC1X 9NG
United Kingdom

Tel: +44 (0)20 7713 5097
Fax: +44 (0)20 7713 8682
sales@artificebooksonline.com
www.artificebooksonline.com

British Library Cataloguing-in-Publication Data. A CIP record for this
book is available from the British Library.

ISBN 978 1 908967 67 1

Designed by Rachel Pfleger at Artifice books on architecture.

Artifice books on architecture is an environmentally responsible
company. *Feilden Clegg Bradley Studios: Learning from Schools* is printed
on sustainably sourced paper.

Cover/ Plymouth School of Creative Arts © Hufton + Crow.